BACK WHEN SAILING
WAS FUN

KEITH LORENCE

STARPATH®

ISBN 978-0-914025-31-3

Published by

Starpath Publications

3050 NW 63rd Street, Seattle, WA 98107

Manufactured in the United States of America

www.starpathpublications.com

This book is dedicated to all of the characters who created this mayhem and made sailing fun for me. I have recounted these stories in the hope that it will inspire you to keep the fun in your sailing. Every time you're out there, remember to smell the mildew.

And especially to Red, whose love, support, drive, and constant editing made this book possible. I love you babe.

Contents

Introduction

The idea for this book came about while 'talking story' with sailing buddies from the past, usually at the bar after a race. I was talking to some of the consummate pranksters of their day and got to thinking what fun sailing used to be compared to what the money-driven programs of today have become. The class of the 60's, 70's, and early 80's spawned some true characters.

These days you would get hauled in for some of the hijinks they pulled off. Remember back when a cop would catch you driving a little tipsy, take your keys, drive you home and tell your parents where to find your car?

This book is a statement about the current state of society as well as what's happened in the world of sailing. Paid professional sailing has put so much pressure on sailors to win that the professionals run from one regatta to the next and don't stop to smell the mildewed sails and have a little fun along the way.

All of these stories are true. I have taken some liberties here and there but, all in all, these events happened as written. Names are generally mentioned in the stories, but when changed, they are changed to protect the guilty. This is not intended to be an autobiography of my experiences. I was there and participated in many of them, but these are also stories related to me from sailors all over.

Most of you reading this have your own stories. Send them to me and they'll be in book two! With your byline,

Keith

Offshore Sailing in Big Waves

Most every offshore sailor has been there, and here are a couple from my own experiences.

The Indian Ocean has the biggest and fastest waves I have ever seen. Big enough to get a Swan 65 up and surfing, but it takes 65 knot winds! Big enough to roll a big heavy Swan 65 upside down and fill it with water. Very cold water, too. Scared the crap out of us as we were sure we were sinking 1,250 miles southwest of Perth. Fortunately for us, we weren't.

For me though, two standout waves come to mind.

One was during the 1977 Transpac. We of the Santa Monica Mafia were sailing on an Eva Hollman 50 footer named *Solution*. That year's race had no moon and very low cloud cover for the second half of the race. It was blowing 30 knots with big seas all day and night. Sometimes we would get a wave that we really wish we hadn't.

I happened to be driving when the "feel" of the wave came upon me. Feel is the only way to put it when it's too dark to even see your nose. Turning down a little, *Solution* took off on a pretty big swell and right in the middle of it, we got a large puff. I clearly recall the boat going over the top and angling downward. I was pressed hard up against the wheel thinking this could really turn out wrong, as it was an older I.O.R. boat. I aimed the boat up a little bit to ensure that when we went down, at least it would be the right way. No pole in the water followed by the inevitable dismasting. We were going quite fast and loud when the off watch raced up on deck to see what the hell was going on. They weren't sleeping anyway, as it was very noisy down below. It turned out that we didn't go down, but big Ben Mitchell asked if we were all right. We said that yes, we were fine, but we wanted to take the spinnaker down anyway as we were soaking wet and more than a little shaken. We found out later that 7 boats had been dismasted that night half way to Hawaii. We sailed four nights with a poled-out jib, only using spinnakers during the day. We did ok, and were the first fifty-footer to break ten days to Hawaii, a total of 2,225 miles.

As in most races there were two watches. We called Benny Mitchell's watch "Benny and the Jets," as he had taken many of the better sailors for his side. My watch was called the "dog watch," because I didn't get the stars.

One of our crew, Bob Buell, slept in the bunk above me and is claustrophobic. Several times during the race he woke up screaming, "I have to get out of here!" then stepped on me trying to escape. I had to soothe him and tell him we were sailing to Hawaii with a bunch of amigos. That seemed to calm him down, and he would go back to sleep. The on-deck watch heard this ruckus and shouted down one of the ports, "Arooo-the dog watch." This happened several times, and we always got, "Arooo-the dog watch rides again" back. It was not really all that fun getting woken up with a foot on your chest. 🐚

The 1979 Fastnet Race

Various reports put the peak winds from 55 to 70 knots in the infamous Fastnet race of 1979. We didn't know how hard it was blowing because our wind gear had been blown off the mast, but 70 knots felt about right.

We rounded Fastnet rock with a triple reef in the main and a storm jib, when a very large wave broke over us and washed us half way to the rock!

It was exceptionally windy by now, and it was hard to steer on the broad reach back to Lands End, England. Later that night when it really got windy, and I made the call for main down in order to concentrate the sail area forward to reduce helm and make driving easier. An hour later, the skipper, my brother, Ed Lorence, came up for his watch and asked why we took the main down. I pointed out to him that it was a mite breezy and thought it was the right call.

My watch wasn't going to be able to sleep anyway, so we went below just to sit inside out of the elements. If they wanted help putting the main back up, we would be happy to come up and help. We came up on watch 4 hours later and the main was still down. I asked Ed why they didn't call us to help put it back up?

"Scared," was the terse reply. It was very windy and rough, and I don't think he had been in this much wind before.

It was getting on toward dawn now, and Ben Mitchell and I, being surfers, were drooling over these waves and the power of 60 knots to get us into them. Ben was driving our Peterson 43 when we eventually decided to go for one. (We were broad reaching, and to take a wave would mean sailing thirty degrees low of course.) We picked one of the smaller waves, probably only a forty footer.

I moved behind him to help hold the tiller, and with storm jib only, off we went. We got this monster and it was all we could do to hold *La Pantera* down. Once again, the off watch came running up on deck with cries of "What the hell's going on out here?" All we could respond with was that we just couldn't resist the wave. As they were all surfers, all they could respond with was, "Nice wave."

To this day, the rudder post is twisted 7 degrees from our battle with the wave.

Later in the morning when we tried to make roll call, we were told to get off the radio as the British coast guard was in full rescue mode. That was our first inclination there were problems out there.

Because we were not able to report in, we found out later that we were reported lost at sea in our California and Seattle newspapers, much to the dismay of our friends and families.

Still am lost at sea, I suppose. ◎

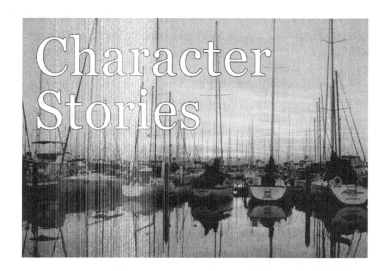

An Alternate Type of Sailing

One of my eccentric friends, Butch Dalrymple-Smith, thought it would be adventurous to reduce sailing to its most simple, rudimentary state. He lived in Sydney, Australia, and had sailed with us in the Congressional Cup in Long Beach, CA three times.

One windy day he brought an ironing board and an umbrella out to North Sydney Heads. He jumped into the water, and using the ironing board as a centerboard held under his arm and the umbrella as a sail, he sailed himself across Sydney harbor to the Royal Sydney Yacht Squadron. It took him a few hours, but he made it without getting run over. Or eaten by sharks.

Butch also designed and built a mechanism which fit onto his sailboard. It had oar locks and fit via a plate that slotted into the centerboard trunk and attached to the mast fitting, making it a rowing sailboard. It was great exercise for the smooth waters of Currabinny in County Cork, Ireland. I rowed it around on Christmas day in 1983 for several hours.

While in Sydney, Butch and I borrowed a 14 foot Cherub dinghy from one of his friends. We waited for a windy day and sailed up to the Navy base at North Sydney Heads and hid in the lee of the ships, pulled the Spinnaker up and paddled out to the wind. Bang! There was lots of wind for a quick slide down the bay, with Butch driving, and me on the trapeze with one foot in the hull strap and one in the transom strap. We were going like the clappers towards Rushcutters Bay. One big problem was that neither of us were dinghy sailors, and had no idea how to come off full hike to get the spin down at a high rate of speed in big breeze.

With a beach coming up rapidly, the only thing we could come up with was to lay the boat down and go for a swim with the sharks. After a nice swim in the warm water of Sydney Harbor, we were able to put the spinnaker away and untangle the rest of the chaos. After cleaning up the mess, Butch and I got back in the boat and sailed away, 100 feet from the beach.

Again, again, and again. ⊗

Baby Changers

My friends Mike and Cecil have children about the same age as my son, Ryan. In fact, when Mike's daughter Shannon was born a few weeks after Ryan. Mike and I decided that they should marry when they became of age so that Mike and I could be related. It was a scary thought for Mike and his wife Suca. That was 28 years ago, and sadly, Ryan and Shannon are still good friends but not married. She did take Ryan to her school in Manzanillo where her family lived for show-and-tell while we were cruising.

Look, I found a gringo!

Mike is from California and has a Mexican wife, Suca. Suca is Spanish for "sugar." Shannon is the spitting image of her mom, a full on Mexican beauty, while his son Shawn is a tow-headed image of his Southern California father. Shawn is also a two time world kite boarding champion.

They now live in Colima, Mexico and the kids are true Mexicans. Mike tries to speak Spanish, but after all these years he's still missing a few words.

One night during Big Boat Series, our crew was at a party at friend Cecil's house. Cecil also had a son in diapers about the same age as Ryan and Shannon, about 3 months old. Mike's daughter and Cecil's son both needed changing, luckily, mine didn't. The moms told the dads to go and do it, as they had been taking care of the kids it all day while we were "out gallivanting about the bay getting our brains beat up in 30 knots of wind."

What no one knew was that Mike had smuggled a handful of guacamole into the bathroom with him. When they came out, he had a spare fresh diaper with him into which he had glopped the Guacamole. Walking into the room, he opened it up and brought out a finger full, tasted it, and proclaimed, "Yup, she's a real beaner" to the disgust of the rest of the partygoers. Cecil was not in on the joke, but never to be out done by Mike, stuck a finger in, pulled out a finger full, and stuck in his mouth. "Yuck" was all we heard from the group as Cecil proclaimed that, "Yes indeed, it does taste like a Mexican baby."

One of our grinders fainted! ᛗ

Boo Boo and the Needle

At Sails By Watts in Torrance, California, the head loft manager, Bob Hanratty, was a wonderful guy and an exceptionally good sail maker. He had the "feel'. He and Kenny Watts made the very best big boat sails in the country. They also made exceptional Star boat sails. They sold their Star sails all over the world. It's a little known fact that Lowell North won his first national championship using sails built by Kenny Watts and Boo. Lowell then took his sails home to San Diego, took them apart and made his own. This was how North Sails got its start.

But this story is about Boo Boo. He began his sailmaking career in San Francisco at a well known loft, and then came to Los Angeles to work with Kenny. He and Kenny taught many of us little kids how to be sailmakers, to analyze sails and build them, recut them, and go on to produce great sails.

One day Boo was working on a sail and needed to sit down on the handwork bench to do some work. He wasn't looking and sat down on a wax ball with a needle stuck in it, which ended up sticking in his butt. All the way. He yowled and screamed until one of the guys came by to grab the twine and pull the needle out. Gross, but true, but he still can sit down to this day!

Boo was also in charge of flying sails prior to shipment. Sails By Watts had two spars, one at 50 feet tall, and an M boat mast at about 120 feet tall, to test sails. We also had a Star boat out back on runners that allowed Kenny to rotate the boat and sails 360 degrees. You could stand right under the sails and check for flaws and shape.

One day after doing a test on a *Windward Passage* spinnaker, Boo forgot to reattach the leeward shroud, (it needed to be released in order to allow the big spinnaker to fly properly). During the night, the offshore breeze came up strongly and blew the 120 foot mast over into the machine shop roof. The tall wooden spar came through with only a minor break, which was easily spliced. We all laughed, as we knew who forgot to re hook the leeward shroud. It made quite a mess of the machine shop, and left splinters everywhere, not to mention the inability to test the rest of the inventory. ᙙ

Clomp Clomp

One of my business friends came up to Seattle and stayed with us on the houseboat during the January boat show many years ago. After the show ended on a Sunday, four of us took my brand new J24 out for some proper yachting. On Lake Union, this means motoring around the lake and hitting all the restaurants along the lake, drinking a little and eating as well.

At the end of the evening, while parking the boat at the house, my friend fell off into some very cold water. (This seems to be a recurring theme at the houseboat). He looked up and mumbled, "Wajabadja?" We all pulled him out of the water, stripped his clothes off, and stuffed him into a hot bath. Then we packed him off to bed. The next day he didn't know why his clothes were all wet. It was a big night!

The following year, another amigo, let's call him "Jeff", happened to be in town, again in January, and wanted to see where his good friend had fallen into the lake. I said, "Right here," and pointed. Jeff said, "Man that water is cold, he must have been frozen!" Later that evening, we thought a little proper yachting would be in order, and invited another friend, Nick, to come along.

Nick was only too happy, as he was a bachelor and looking for something fun to do. He lived on his own forty foot sailboat up the lake.

We four went on our merry way to several restaurants.

While parked on a guest dock before leaving one restaurant, looking in through the windows, Nick and Jeff spied two nice looking women and decided to run back in and recruit them as deckhands. I had the engine running and was watching the goings-on while my crew pointed to the J24. We watched as the ladies shook their heads no. Dejected, my crew turned to leave when two other women at the next table stood up and said, "Take us!" Well why not? That is, until "Jeff" looked down and found that one of them had two foot and ankle casts. It was her first night out after double Achilles tendon surgery and she was looking to have some fun. Well, ok.

We puttered along to another watering hole and, when we hit the dock, Jeff said, "We'll be along in a few." A few turned into several Irish Coffees for us, with no sign of them. We finally went down to the boat and found just what we expected. It was getting late so we motored home.

Then the outboard caught fire. Fortunately, we had a bucket in the cockpit, and were able to get the fire out.

We sailed the rest of the way back home and, right at the turn to my dock, Jeff fell off the bow. Right at the same place where his amigo had fallen the year before! Once again, a hot bath and wet clothes.

Nick drove his girl home to his own boat, while Jeff stayed on the houseboat with us. Before going to bed, Jeff asked me for my car keys saying he didn't want to wake up to his girl, that she only lived a mile or two away. It should be easy to find, even though he didn't know is way around Seattle. All night long all I could hear was the "clomp, clomp" of her casts hitting the guest bedroom window. At one especially active point, I had to yell out, "Don't break my window!!"

I heard the front door shut around 4 a.m. and they clomped down the dock to the car. Jeff returned three hours later. For only a one mile jaunt, 3 hours seemed a bit long.

When he came home, I saw he was in just his underwear as the rest of his clothes were still wet. He told us about his long journey for a ten minute trip to her house, and getting lost on the way home. It turned out to be a three hour tour around Seattle! He had apparently driven around the whole time trying to find his way back. It was a harrowing experience because he was almost out of gas, unable to stop for directions because he was in just his undies. And the cops were not an option with him in undies at that time of the morning.

We all had a good laugh over this, but at least she didn't break my window.

And he got to see where his buddy fell in the lake firsthand.
◉

Phil Holland—Sea Dude

I first met Phil Holland in Honolulu after the 1973 Transpac. He is a New Zealander, and the brother of well known yacht designer Ron Holland. Phil had sailed Transpac on *New World*, an unusual 70-foot schooner that finished just in front of us on our C&C 61 *Robon*.

One morning we awoke (crews still slept on boats back when sailing was fun) to crashing and banging on New World. They were preparing for Phil's wedding day. It was said that Phil needed a green card to stay in the US, while the bride wanted a card to work in New Zealand. The crew of *Robon* chipped in with a bit of sweat equity and we found ourselves, as fellow sailors and next door neighbors, invited to the wedding. It was a grand affair that included many of the Transpac luminaries, plus a bunch of prominent local sailors. When it was time for the wedding, we swooped across on halyards in our cleanest shorts and crew shirts, decked out in leis, and ready to attend a very nice affair catered by Primo Beer and Pattie's Chinese Kitchen from the Ala Moana center.

The party quickly deteriorated into a typical Kiwi drinking affair, during which the bride and groom were ceremoniously tossed into the Ala Wai Yacht Harbor, a festering hotbed of staph infection. Shortly, all of the sailors and guests were swimming in the harbor with their bottles of Primo held high and their staph infections forming.

It was here that I first met a South African named Richard Bertie, aka Thirsty, who had sailed on a boat called *Stormy*. Thirsty has since gone on to be a well known sailor and boat builder in South Africa and after the swim, he happily showed me how to tie a Turks head around my wrist. I kept this Turks head on my wrist for 5 years including the round the world race, in remembrance of this fine adventure. A grand time was had by all and the party went long into the night. The morning dawned with hangovers and lost sailors. I believe this was around the time when owners first began giving out crew shirts to help the local police know where to return stray drunken sailors.

The next morning the motley crews all woke up with big heads. When the first hair of the "Primo" dog kicked in, we sobered up enough to realize that all those cuts and scratches from being pushed, tossed or just drunkenly falling into the festering Ala Wai, had blossomed into full fledged staph infections overnight.

Enter Dr. Bill Sullivan, aka Blue Willie to those of us who sailed with him. He owned a 42-footer, and his crew had made up much of the Ala Wai swim team. He was feeling sorry for us poor kids, and set up shop on his boat the next morning. The line formed well up the dock for a shot of penicillin and some sort of hog's wart to fend off the ugly infections forming on our young bodies. It is unknown whether the Primo or the O'Kolehau had any effect on the antibiotics.

Phil Holland, in typical Phil Holland fashion, was Teflon. The next morning he had no festering sores and a pretty new bride whom we all coveted.

A few years later in the Admiral's Cup of 1977, Phil tossed his hotel room phone out of his window because of frustration with the English operators. I was young and impressionable and followed suit. Two months later I received a bill from the hotel for my phone. Phil, with devilish forethought, had put his room in one of the other crewmember's names and was never caught. Bastard.

On an evening during the 1974 Cowes race week, our crew was having beers at the Island Sailing Club. Phil drunkenly came up to us and asked if we wanted to go with him on the Ballyhoo chase boat up the river to the casino for some fun. We all came to the same conclusion: bad idea. Stay where we were and we could walk home later.

For those of you who have never been to Cowes, there is a ferry that uses chains to pull itself, with a full load of cars and passengers, across a narrow part of the river. In the timeless spirit of cars trying to beat a railroad train across the tracks, Phil tried to beat the chain ferry with the boat's Whaler. It didn't go well for him, as the chains get pulled fairly tightly and close to the surface. He got hung up on one of them. The ferry ran over his Whaler sinking it, and left Phil hanging on to the bow of the ferry which was about to beach itself in order to offload the cars. So there was Phil hanging from the bow and the landing was coming up fast. Suffice it to say, he made it. He had to let go and swim away from the ferry before he was crushed, and then swim back across the channel. Next thing we knew, he walked into the Island Sailing Club soaking wet, telling stories about his brush with death.

I had the misfortune to be in Cork, Ireland where Phil, Ron and Butch lived designing racers and cruisers for Ron Holland yacht design. It was the Christmas and New Year's holidays in 1983 and it fell upon Phil to cook the Christmas leg of lamb. In fine Irish tradition, he put the roast in the oven and we all took off for a little pubbing while the ladies stayed behind and prepared the rest of the meal. We made it back a few hours later, in time for the Lamb dinner, but Phil may have been over served just a touch. He pulled the roast out of the oven to have a look at it when it slid off the pan and onto the floor. I was the only other person in the kitchen. We looked at each other and almost in unison said, "I didn't see anything, did you?" Three second rule in effect here. A quick wash and all was well with the lamb. We all had a fine Christmas dinner with all the trimmings in Curribinny, Cork, Ireland.

The next day, the group went on a fine adventure to Ron's summer house in the south of Ireland for New Year. More pubbing along the way led us to Skibbereen, a small southern Irish town. Phil was pitching darts just for fun when two locals came up to him and asked if he wanted a match? Why sure, it was the holidays after all, and when in Rome. So Phil and Butch prepared to lose. They threw for which team starts, and Phil got lucky and won the first throw.

In a string of pure dumb luck, he ran up a whole lot of points, and Phil and Butch won the match over the locals on their own turf. The locals were surprised, but very good natured and bought us all pints. And that is how Butch and Phil became the winter darts champions of Skibbereen in 1983.
※

R.P.B.

An old friend, Roy Cundiff, had a Cal 27. We sailed against him all the time with our Cal 30 and he usually won. Beating up on us poor little kids. Come on!

On his transom he had the letters "R.P.B. in bold size. Being junior sailors, we tentatively walked up to one of the great sailors and sail makers in southern California and asked him what it meant. He looked over at us kids and said,

Rape Pillage and Burn!

We sixteen year olds could only shake our heads at this old guy! He was having a good time at our expense. Wonderful guy to us juniors, he was always there to help us learn.

R.P.B. 🌀

Rocket Man

We were sailing *Taxi Dancer* in the MEXORC in Manzanillo. The regatta was sailed out of Las Hadas, the hotel made famous by Bo Derek in the movie "10". After a day of sailing, the boats med tie to the quay in the harbor. On Taxi Dancer, we tied up to a large power yacht that Mike took care of and sat under the canopy to hide from the sun while sipping our wine. The racers from other boats would wander up to the pool and jump in to cool off, rinse off the sunscreen and have some drinks.

One day after sailing I asked Mike if he had any rockets. "Of course I do. I just got in a new batch!" he said. "Great, bust 'em out!" I replied. He went below and returned with two four foot long bombers. "Anyone have a match?" he asked. No one on the boat had a match as no one smokes anymore so Mike asked a passing Federally (police officer) if he had a light for his cigar. The fed looked up and said, "Senor Farley, no rockets!"

"No, of course not," he replied, "just a cigar." The fed lit Mike's cigar and proceeded out to the end of the quay on his patrol, or perhaps he was just looking at the boats, then walked back past toward the pool waving his finger at Mike.

Mike waited an appropriate length of time until the fed was out of sight, stepped down onto the quay, held this giant sucker in his left hand, then lit it off with his cigar and aimed it above the pool. The rocket leapt out of his hand and took off

14

toward the pool, exploding about 20 feet above it. Palm trees surround the pool with an island in the middle of it. Iguanas live in the trees, and swim back and forth from the island. As my fellow racer and friend Bill described it, when the bomb went off, it began raining Iguanas. One fell into his Gin and Tonic! Mike blew the iguanas out of the trees! 🐚

More Mike and the Rockets

One night after racing in Newport Beach, and several drinks, Mike and his crowd decided that it would be fun to send some rockets up the fireplace chimney of their beach house.

These things are 1/4 sticks of dynamite rockets. He let fly with a few, lighting up the night sky in spectacular fashion, and then headed for the bathroom.

While he was out of the room, one of his really good friends closed the flue in the fireplace and then suggested that it would be fun for the crowd to go outside to watch them fly. Mike stayed in and fired one more off, which promptly bounced off the flue and back into the living room and chased Mike all over the room till it exploded next to a chandelier.

I think he still has trouble with that ear. He says he does.

The massive explosion took the rigs out of two model boats, blew the pictures off the walls, and set off the smoke alarms. Chandelier glass flew all over the room. It took a week to clean up the shards of glass. The crowd was rolling with laughter in the sand on the beach outside.

Before the police came, Cecil took off with his wife Alyson, but before he left, he had the courtesy to steal the electric meter. This left the house with no lights for two days before he brought the meter back.

What a night it was... A lethal mix of alcohol, weed, and various other banned substances.

Luckily, we are all still alive. 🐚

A Surprise Going Away Party!

Several of we sailing friends have a madcap buddy who goes by the name of Michael Pope. In the 70's, he had a series of racing yachts named *Vatican* in Vancouver, BC, and campaigned them very successfully.

He had, and maybe still has, a habit of living off his friend's generosity, and exchanges his high-quality woodwork in return for the favors we give him.

In 1979, I had to go off to some regatta in the UK, and it fell upon Mike to care for my houseboat in Seattle. While I was away, he promised to build a skylight over the bathroom. All went well and it was beautiful, as he is a master carpenter. He's just not a master finisher. I returned home from the Fastnet race to find a nice skylight, but no lid. I scrambled to find some visqueen, and as it was Seattle, it was going to rain soon.

He had also built an addition to the houseboat to accommodate a captain's bed for him to camp in. This addition would eventually become my son's bedroom. Michael even threatened to put in a separate door for himself. But after 6 months he became like an old fish. My wife really wanted him out so she came up with a novel way to lose Michael. She catered quite a party, and invited all of our sailing friends. When Michael came home that evening, there was a roaring party going on. When he walked in we all yelled, "Surprise!!" He was a little unsure about the surprise, but went along with it for a while until he finally asked, "What's the surprise?" We all said in unison, " It's a surprise going away part". Tentatively, he asked, "Whose?" and we all, again in unison, said, "Yours." Not much to be said after that, and he left shortly thereafter. A surprise going away party.

Perhaps some of you can use this. 🔗

Mike and the Bird

I had a parrot named Streaker, (because he had no feathers when we got him) and for reasons unknown, he hated Michael with a passion. I put Streaker's perch right by the door to the head. When Michael would get up in the night to pee, Streaker would lunge at him, often inflicting damage to his ears. One day, in an act of revenge, Michael pinned an eight by ten photo of himself on the wall behind the perch to piss the bird off. It worked, because Streakier was never able to relax, but he was eventually able to reach the picture and tear it to shreds. We awoke one morning to find the shredded pieces of Mike's picture on the floor.

I had to give the bird away when my son was born to ensure that he could grow up with 10 fingers. Nasty birds those Mexican double yellow heads.

In 1994 Michael was off cruising, and was caught in a typhoon off Fiji and reported missing at sea. I happened to see the report in a Honolulu newspaper and called the local newspaper in Fiji. I asked the editor about him, and if he had been found. There was a long pause before the editor said, "Unfortunately, yes." It seems that his boat had been rolled, lost its mast and suffered serious damage.

And that Mike was not the most popular man in Fiji for political reasons.

He had broken ribs and a number of other broken bones, and his hand had lain on the floor in battery acid for two days. The battery acid had the curious effect of burning off his warts! The Fijian Coast Guard finally found him, a broken wreck, and brought him back to the island. When he was deported to Seattle, my wife and I threw him a wake and invited all his friends. There were only two of us who knew he was in town. We invited him to his own wake on friend Davey's houseboat. We thought of it as a sort of Finnegan's wake.

Mike showed up, to the surprise of all but the two of us. Eventually we had to give him another surprise going away party! 🐚

Christmas Dinner in Mexico

Aqui No Mas and two of our cruising buddy boats sailed from Chacala, North of Puerto Vallarta, Mexico to La Cruz De Xuanacastle on December 24th 1997. This is a trip of about 30 miles.

We were in a hurry to make it in time for Christmas Eve, and had a lovely sail in 15 knots of wind, averaging about nine knots over the course. Bandaras bay off of Puerto Vallarta is beautiful, and teams with sea life. Porpoise, sunfish, and many other fishy things, including sea snakes, were visible. Bandaras also has several great surf breaks of which we availed ourselves.

It was a normal 80 degree December day, with clear Blue skies when we sailed into La Cruz around 3 p.m, just in time for a refreshing swim followed by a cool fresh water rinse. The group decided that we should go ashore in search of something special for Christmas Eve dinner. The only restaurant even close to open was the "Bedrock Café." Of course, we sent our best Fred Flintstone emissary inside to scope out the possibilities. He asked the owner if it was possible to have Christmas Eve dinner. The owner said they were closed for the holiday. That is, until our emissary mentioned that there were 10 of us. "Well of course we can serve you! But all we have are spare ribs. Will that be OK?" the proprietor asked. After boat rations for two weeks anything sounded good to us and we all agreed that ribs for Christmas Eve dinner would be most excellent. As luck would have it, the Café even had a pool table!

It turned out that he was from Chicago and was just hanging on business-wise and 10 people for dinner was a Christmas Eve present for him. We wound up with a meal that never ended: lots of Coronas, Tequila, and unending piles of ribs. A true Christmas present for all involved. The kids each got a beer and played pool till midnight when we retired to our respective yachts, but not before asking if we could return for a Christmas dinner the next day.

"But of course, what would you like for your Christmas dinner? How about a giant platter of fresh shrimp? Is 5 o'clock okay?" he asked. "Perfect," said we.

We had Christmas morning mass on a Cal 46 named *Morning Star*, which we had renamed Morning Bar. There we sang and told of our blessings and of being in a Mexican paradise on Christmas day. Then we all jumped onto *Aqui No Mas*, the biggest boat, and went for a sail and a swim.

When we rolled into the Bedrock Café in the late afternoon, we found a giant mountain of shrimp just off of the boat. It was a scrumptious dinner, and we played lots of pool, drank more Coronas, and then swam back to the boats to play cards all night. And then swam some more.

The little town was all shut down on Christmas night; lights out, town dark. La Cruz is what we called a "Pig and Chicken" town. It's all dirt roads full of chickens, roosters and all manner of animals running around loose. With just a few small abborotes, and a motel, it was truly a wonderful Christmas away from the hype of the U.S.A. 🐚

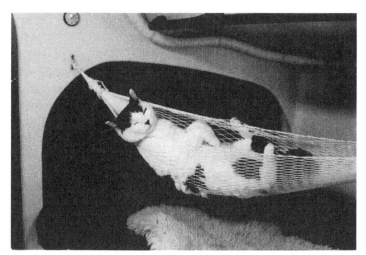
Pinto in Mexican mode

Christmas Parties

Every year at Sobstad Sails Seattle, we sponsored a Christmas party at the loft. Some of them were heroic. We invited all of our customers, family and friends. Food was catered- the usual carrots, celery, cauliflower, broccoli, cheese, dips, spiral-sliced ham, and the like. It was a gathering of sailing buddies talking about the past year of sailing and epic adventures. Wine flowed, beer spilled, and a good time was had by all.

I bought a few new trash cans every year just for the occasion knowing that, inevitably, the party would deteriorate into a food fight. The group – customers and employees alike would square off on opposite sides of the loft and fire carrots, celery and whatever else they could lay their hands on at the other side. But never the spiral-sliced ham. I was always careful to hide the scissors and seam rippers. We would find these foody looking things for years behind boxes and sewing machine tables.

Sobstad Seattle seemed to be a fertile forest, as there were always employees' kids running around the loft. We even had a Johnny jump up permanently attached to the ceiling, as many of the moms worked too.

During one particularly raucous Christmas party, we put the kids into boxes and dragged them around the floor in circles till they were dizzy. Then the contest began and we flung the box spinning across the floor as far as we could with kids inside. The loft was 100 feet long, so they spun quite far and came out very dizzy. We called it The Kid Toss.

A few years later at another Christmas party, we were adding space to the loft and needed to knock down a wall. After checking with the builder for electrical issues, I bought two sledge hammers. I charged a dollar a swing (to help with the party costs) and most everyone had a good try at knocking the wall down; like ringing the bell at the fair and, lo and behold, we had a bigger sail loft! As many as 100 people would pass through during the evening, so there was no shortage of swingers.

Ahhh, the loft parties... 🪢

"Jeff" and Randi Streak the Party

After one the Christmas parties at the Seattle loft, we all adjourned to Fred's nearby apartment for some post party libations, good fun and sailing camaraderie. There were about 15 people there, just having a good time.

At one point, someone noticed that Randi and "Jeff" had disappeared. As both were married, and not to each other, we all noticed, and commented curiously as it was a small apartment.

"Jeff" and Randi had snuck off to the small bathroom and hit upon a plan.

Streak the party! But they needed a backup plan.

They threw their clothes out the bathroom window, looked at each other and said, "Now there's the point of no return," gave each other a big hug and streaked to the front door in front of us all, praying that the door wasn't locked.

It wasn't, and they made it to the door and outside. They returned sheepishly a few minutes later fully clothed to the cheers of all.

Fred, being Fred, announced that the party was over, and we all had to go home. Being 6'6" and 250 pounds, we were not going to argue with him and so we all left.

Fred later disappeared and hasn't been heard from in 15 years. 🐚

Crabs!

Not those kind! The Dungeness type.

We were at a crew party at Ron's house for the end of the year fiesta in Tacoma, WA. About thirty of us there having a good time. Many were sitting in the hot tub, some playing pool, and others just sitting and chatting, when in walked Breck with a big bag of Dungeness crabs. Breck surveyed the situation and asked Ron's wife if she had a pot big enough for the big bag'O'crabs. She said not one big enough for all of those. Breck promptly walked over to where were sitting in the hot tub drinking, and dumped them in the 105 degree water. We all jumped out of the water to avoid being pinched and sat on the edge watching the things slow cook in our hot tub. After fifteen minutes or so, he reached in and we all had a nice crab dinner. Crabs, ala hot tub. A truly unusual way of preparing them. Hard on the toes though.

Nobody went home that night. Too much inebriation to drive. One character, one Michael P was found naked under the piano the next morning by the owner's wife. He was sleeping on a sheepskin rug. Still drunk.

If you are going to cook crabs in a hot tub, allow a little extra time. 🦀

Windward Passage and Kialoa

The epic food fights during the pre race party before Transpac between *Kialoa* and *Windward Passage* are legend. The two crews were usually seated a convenient potato toss apart. With these two arch rivals, it had to happen. Especially with the characters sailing on these two boats.

I can vividly recall sitting at our table, it had to have been 1971, or 1973.

Spuds flew, slathered in butter, over our heads. Soon, the room erupted in flying food, and we were all unwilling participants in a typical *WP/Kialoa* brawl.

It was too long ago, back when sailing was fun, to remember all of it. 🦀

Shenandoah

Another one of my favorites was the 1982 Big Boat Series in San Francisco. We were sailing a Ron Holland forty named *Shenandoah*.

Our resident I.B.N.A. rep did a great job with the boat, but we had an only ok regatta. Our fault, but he did a wonderful job with the crew dinner.

We wound up at a small Middle Eastern restaurant named Mamounias.

It was clear this would be an unusual night when we were given shower size towels upon entry, shown to a Cobra sized bread basket, and told to pick as many of the buns as we wanted. We were then shown to a room with a low table, and a ledge around the perimeter. When our menus arrived, hand written on blank paper, we found several choices. Most everyone opted for chicken, with some at Lamb. The chicken came whole, and we soon learned why the beach towels. There was no silverware, you tore the chicken apart by hand and used the towels as napkins, albeit large ones. The food was great, and we all had a good laugh and good crew camaraderie at the setting.

There was another big basket of bread rolls in the room, and they became missiles. Then the chicken wings started to fly. Then the vegetables and all hell broke out.

Other crews in the restaurant came into our room and joined in with their food. It was a hoot, and we had to get more towels, as well a Laundromat. 🐚

Taxi Crew Dinner, Take One

The same year that Mike had his rockets in Manzanillo, we had a *Taxi Dancer* crew dinner at a small restaurant on the main drag in town. It was a great crew dinner with about 30 people. All were having a great time, drinking and partying... until the potato incident.

I was near one end of the table, and Norman was about in the middle. I thought it would be fun to hit him with a baked potato slathered in butter. I launched it and was on target when Cecil leaned forward. Cecil is one of the guys that ate glasses, and he wasn't happy about a baked potato to the head. As you can imagine, during a Taxi party, things like this had the potential to spiral out of control fast. Cecil retaliated in kind but missed me and hit Mike. Mike doesn't back down for anyone and he fired some fish at Cecil, missed and hit one of the other crewmember's wife.

Katie, bar the door, the fight was on.

Food started flying off plates and into whoever happed to be in the flight path.

Chairs flew across the table and over the bar. Cecil went into the kitchen, opened the freezer and grabbed several red snappers (huachinango) and stuffed them down the front of several women's low cut dresses.

Food and chairs were flying everywhere. All of the other customers fled and the Taxi crew continued on like this for 30 minutes or so.

All the while, the restaurant owner sat with his wife at a nearby table writing on a tablet. Every time a fish, a chair or anything else of value flew by, he would duly note it on the pad. They were both thinking that they had sold a lot more than food that night.

Mitch, the owner of *Taxi Dancer* finally said, "Okay boys, you've had your fun, go to the bar for one last round while I sit with the owner." Mitch and the restaurant owner came to a settlement with which they both seemed happy, and which included the restaurant owner and his wife sailing with us the next day.

The rest of the crew drank up until they were done, and then most piled into the van for the trip back to Las Hadas, and home.

Norman and I rode with Mike, the blond, and Suca and along the way we picked up 3 smoge poges, the type they use to keep orchards from freezing in winter. In Mexico, they use them for road guidance. We put them on top of Mike's truck, and beat it back toward Las Hadas. On the way there is a hill and at the top of the hill, we set the poges out in the street and waited until our fellow travelers came to the top. We waved them down to stop, and when they did, we ripped our shorts down and BA'd them. To howling hoots of laughter from all.

That night I came down with food poisoning and spent the night throwing up. I was able to get down to the little hotel store for a bottle of water; just barely though. I stayed in bed until late the next morning before wandering down to the boat. The crew was rigging up so I went over to the grass, saying, "Wake me in time." It became time and I was able to get to the boat.

On the way out to the start, there was a large helium balloon with a camera shooting the boats near the start line. Farley thought it would be fun to shoot it down and brought out a couple of his rockets.

Standing on the transom, he fired one off toward the balloon, where it exploded just a little too far away to do any damage. The next one blew a little early, and was captured by the camera.

Just before the start, Mitch said, "Keith, you do the start." I was horrified, as I didn't think I was up for it in a fleet of ten seventy-footers, being sick and all. But he insisted. We were close on points to another seventy for second place, and needed to win the start. Coming into the crowd on port with one minute to go, at ten knots, I swung into a hole ahead and to leeward of the boat we needed to beat. It was perfect, till I fell down. I was drained. Norman grabbed the wheel and said, "Hang in there big boy" and proceeded to finish off a near perfect start, just under the enemy.

Just another day in paradise for Taxi and the gang! 🐚

Taxi Dinner, Take Two

A few years later during Big Boat Series on *Taxi Dancer*, we had a crew dinner at a well-known Italian restaurant in San Francisco's North Beach, Emilio's.

We all had a fabulous, festive dinner downstairs in the wine cellar. About 25 people were seated around a long table, enjoying good crew comradery and good food. Nobody had broken anything – yet. No fish had been thrown, so all was cool. Dessert appeared along with several rounds of Irish coffees, it was San Francisco, after all, and things were going well for us on the race course.

Eventually, as it often does with the Taxi group, things went south. Cecil and Mike Farley made a bet. Who could eat his Irish coffee glass the fastest? The race was on. I don't remember who won but I am quite certain the waiter was horrified at these two big guys eating their glasses.

Things went downhill pretty fast after this, and after the Manzanillo food fight, the owner decided that we should leave before more damage could ensue. Good thought! So we all filed up the stairs and out onto the street. I was about the fifth person out the door following a tall young blond woman, who is famous in her own way and a good sailor to boot.

Outside, there was a street person walking toward our group and the tall blond grabbed his baseball cap from atop his head. He totally freaked and yelled, "Give my hat back, you bitch!" She did and apologized, trying to calm him down, but to no avail. He kept coming for her and grabbing at her. By now the rest of the crew had made it to the street. One of the crew was an L.A. cop. Arnie grabbed this guy and held him in a police strangle hold till he almost blacked out. Arnie then walked him across the street, and tossed him into a row of Hells Angels bikes in front of a biker bar, knocking them down like dominoes. Just as the bikers came out to see what the commotion was, a taxi pulled up. Three of us jumped in and told the driver to not spare the horses, but get us to the Buena Vista quickly, where we all had some more Irish coffees. Then the rest of the crew showed up to fill us in on how the bikers beat the crap out of the bum. One came after the L.A. cop, but it didn't go too well for the biker.

Just another Taxi Crew dinner, back when sailing was fun.
🐚

Anonymous Amigo

During the Midsummer's Regatta at San Diego Yacht Club, it had to be about 1969, we were sailing on a Cal 34 in their national championships.

After sailing on Saturday, Stu and I thought it would be fun to get our friend drunk. Being 18 and unable to buy drinks at the bar, we raided the visiting boats from our yacht club, Cabrillo Beach YC, for all the alcohol we could find. We started with Cal 40 row and worked our way down, all the while filling our friend with whatever we could find and helping ourselves as well to keep pace.

Needless to say, we drank more than enough to get us drunk. Walking through the parking lot of the SDYC, we spied the 120 foot mast on top of the North Sails loft next door. It looked like a fun thing to climb so we walked over to the loft with that as our goal. Fortunately for us, the gate was locked and we were too drunk to climb over it. God forbid if we had made it, we might be dead today, or at best, we'd have been arrested.

Denied access to the towering mast, we staggered back to SDYC where our nameless friend passed out in his VW bug, puking all over the inside of his car. Stu and I made it back to the boat where we quickly passed out in our bunks.

Waking up the next morning to the sound of the owner pounding on the deck, we found that our friend had made it down to the boat and was curled up in a fetal position, freezing cold in the cockpit. "Come on boys," the owner said, "We're winning the Nationals and I'm buying breakfast in the club restaurant, and by the way, what happened to him?" No comment. Stu and I didn't really feel like eating, but felt it only right to go with the owner. Our friend, on the other hand, was less than optimistic about food. But what the hell, we were eighteen and bulletproof, right?

At breakfast, pancakes sounded like a good sponge for the poisons we had ingested the night before. Half way through breakfast, sitting across from our nameless friend, I noticed him looking a little queasy. I wasn't feeling so great myself, but apparently not as bad as him because just then he leaned over his plate of pancakes and ralphed in them, then politely put his napkin over the plate and walked away to safer grounds— like the bathroom.

Stu and I had to look away to avoid the same catastrophe when the owner asked, "You boys have some fun last night? Well, let's just pretend this never happened."

Then the waiter came over to pick up the plates and stack them up... well, you can imagine; enough said. That day we watched the first man land on the moon on one of those new fangled boat TV's.

And we won the Cal 34 Nationals too.

Hungover to beat the band. 🐚

Big Boat Off Days

In the old days of Big Boat Series, Burke Sawyer, the owner of Sails by Watts, would organize some entertainment for us all. In the 60's, 70's and early 80's, the BBS was sailed Sunday,

Monday, off day Tuesday, and then afternoon businessman's special start Wednesday, Thursday off, and finish off racing Friday and Saturday.

On the Tuesday, Sails by Watts would charter a bus and about 50 of us would head off to Healdsburg in the Sonoma valley to pick up canoes, paddles and life jackets. Then we proceeded to Asti, a winery about 20 miles north through the Sonoma Valley, to pick up wine. Asti sold wine with handles on the gallon bottles so we could tie a spinnaker retrieval line to it and hang it over the side of the canoe to keep it cool in the 90-degree heat.

After purchasing wine, we launched our canoes, one guy and one girl to a boat, and proceeded down the river—usually naked. By the end of the day, we usually had sunburns in places we didn't really want sunburns.

The residents in the houses along the river never liked Big Boat Series, as they had to hide their children while 30 canoes full of naked, drunken adults floated past. We sailors would pound the paddles on the floor of the canoes in what we thought was an Indian drumbeat. Some years the river was low and we had to ford our way across the sandbars, much to the dismay of the locals. When we arrived at the canoe center some 4 hours later—sunburned, drunk and disorderly—the bus would take us to a fancy restaurant for a feast. Unfortunately, by this time it was too late for some and they missed the feasting. That was our Tuesday.

The Thursday of the BBS was reserved for a trip to Napa and some wine tasting. One of our crew owned a chain of high end restaurants in Los Angeles and could get us into wineries the average tourist couldn't get into. We did find some nice boutique wineries.

One Thursday our group went up in my Sobstad loft van in a caravan of perhaps ten cars, trucks, and rental cars. Our first stop was usually Domain Chandon for some Champagne and breakfast. Our next stop was Beaulieu Vineyards. It's a nice place and open to the public and they served all you wanted, but they wouldn't let Mikey in because he had no shoes on. He said, "No problem" and went across the street to the market and bought two boxes of sugar cubes. He dumped the cubes out and put the boxes on his feet. That seemed to work, but to the winery's later dismay, he and Cecil were later found under one of the giant wine vats with the tap open, guzzling wine straight from it. This was back in the day when they would pour wine-as much as you wanted. After a day of debauchery, we would return to San Francisco-with luck.

One year during BBS, shortly after Mount St Helens blew, I had some fun. I had been sailing in eastern Washington where I had bought a Tupperware container and filled it with volcanic ash. If you ever wind up with a jar of ash, just hold it out the open side door of the van. The stuff is so light that it blows all over, obscuring the sight of the cars behind you, especially your wine soaked friends. 🐚

Ed and the Keg

In 1962, my brother Ed was recruited to take care of me while our parents were on an extended trip to the East coast. He was eighteen years old and I was eleven. He is an excellent sailor, by the way.

After school one day he asked if I would like to go for a drive in his new car. "Yes!" I said enthusiastically. It turned out to be some 1940's car that he had picked up from a friend, but it seemed to run well and get him around. Until he took me out for a ride and broke down far away from home. Shit. We had to walk 4 miles through the snow to get home and call a tow truck. There are a lot of tow trucks in Los Angeles, so it worked out OK.

Ed used to chase me around the center wall of our house but I was smaller, faster, and lighter than he and could usually escape him. I would grab the molding at the corners and swing around them to accelerate and gain some distance. One time he came around a few paces behind, grabbed the molding and it came off in his hand. He took a header into the next wall and fell down in a daze. I scampered over to him, laughed, then took off before he could get up and grab me.

While the parents are away, the kids will play. So once, when Ed was about 18, he had a party for his sailing buddies at our house. Somehow he managed to score a keg of beer. The fun part was when he was carrying the keg into the house. He dropped it on his foot. He broke a bunch of bones in his foot and he had to get one of his friends to take him to the doctor. His other sailing buddies stayed behind with me and we laughed and laughed. Even though I was younger, they were my friends too and most still are today. I was like a little brother to them.

When the cast came off two months later, he sailed a 5 meter—yes a 5 meter—in a race to Catalina Island with some of these same sailing buddies. I suspect they probably won because Ed is a really good sailor. After they picked up their mooring in Catalina, they went up to the small restaurant for dinner and drinks. He knew the manager there and was allowed in the bar.

While they were there, another patron hitched his chair back to stand up and put the chair leg on my brothers newly healed foot and sat down. Ouch! The bones re-broke, resulting in another cast for eight weeks.

My mother never found out how he did it. It was a brotherly secret to the end. But I know. 🐚

Dinghy Movies

While cruising in Mexico, one of the larger boats had a portable television set aboard. They also had a lot of VCR movies, as did many of the other cruisers. This boat also had a microwave for popcorn for the masses.

Once a week we would have movie night. The TV set would be brought up on deck and put in a prominent place. The other cruisers would come over and tie off the transom for a movie and popcorn night.

The price of admission was a bottle of wine or a six pack. Forty of us would sit there in our dinghies whiling the hours, away drinking wine watching the movie. And just generally chattering.

Some nights there were so many, people would have to join others in their dinghies up front to see. Peeing over the side was a don't look don't tell event.

Movie night became quite popular, and was looked forward to all week. A debate on which movie to watch would be debated on the beach in the afternoon while drinking chilled Pacifico's. Favorites were Caddyshack and Happy Gilmore. When the movie was over, if no one had another movie, it became a pool party where clothes came off and everyone went for a swim in the 80' water.

It fell upon the organizer to replace the TV set back to its home and clean the boat. The cruisers, in the best greenpeace movement, had to clear the floating bottles from the water while the rest swam ashore for more Pacificos. We had as many as 20 dinghies rafted up, many empty as the late comers moved up to forward seats.

All in all, an impromptu blue/green carpet performance.
᠙

Center Seat Roulette

The Carr trophy is a West Coast challenge between yacht clubs. The skipper has to be over 50 years of age and the crew over 40. San Diego Yacht Club was invited to sail the regatta in San Francisco in Cal 20's.

As the skipper, I invited two prominent fellow San Diego YC members as crew. Staff commodore Ken Bertino, our protocol officer, was in charge of keeping us from embarrassing SDYC, and Scot Tempesta of Sailing Anarchy fame, was our publicist. To Ken's dismay, Scot and I felt that it would be fun to have a running commentary of our adventures on the Sailing Anarchy website. On SA, we reported all the blows, miscues, and follies.

The fun began at SDYC the morning of our flight to San Francisco with a late taxi. We naturally had to wander to the dining area for coffee where we found the bar open. Bloody Mary's? But of course! Off to a good start already!

Getting onto the airplane went smoothly enough. We stopped at an airport store to pick up sandwiches, because Southwest Airlines is festival seating and doesn't provide food. First come, first served seating.

Scot took the window seat and I took the aisle leaving the center seat open. Ken sat across from us on the aisle. Anytime a man would come down the aisle, Scot and I would lean together in deep conversation. A cute girl? We leaned apart leaving the center seat wide open. This didn't go as well as we had hoped, but we did wind up with an empty center seat. Sadly, no cute girl.

Then the flight attendant showed up to close the overhead stowage. My sandwich fell out on her head. She looked at us with a smirk and said, "You're the two scaring off the girls from the center seat," which was indeed the last thing we wanted. She held up the sandwich, looked at Scot and said, "I suppose this is yours?" It was mine but I kept mum. Our protocol officer, Ken, was rolling his eyes at us by now, fearing what more the weekend could bring.

We eventually arrived in Oakland, rented a car and drove over to Golden Gate Yacht Club where we found no activity. We wandered the short walk to Saint Francis YC for a beer. At STFYC, like many Yacht Clubs, they require you to sign in, in order to buy drink tickets. Staff commodore Ken went to the front desk and asked for a guest card. The club manager asked him for five dollars for the guest card. "Five dollars? For what?" Ken asked. "A guest card that allows you to purchase expensive drinks and take home unused tickets", replied the manager. Ken paid, and standing behind him I casually mentioned that any Saint Francis YC member should be asked to pay ten dollars for a guest card at San Diego Yacht Club.

This went over about as well as you would expect, but we got our card anyway. The three of us went into the casual side of the bar area which is partitioned off from the main bar. We were there sipping wine when the waiters brought out the mini pizza hors d'oeuvres and placed them on a table by the window. "How nice of them," we thought, "thinking of their guests."

There were no other people in the room so we helped ourselves, and cleaned off the tray, leaving a stack of small plates on our table. Soon the partition was opened and the beautiful people of the YC roamed over to graze. Seeing an empty tray, they looked over at us and noticed the tall stack of empty plates on our table. There were a lot of glares from the debs, as I'm sure they were "simply famished" and pining for the pizza slices. They got lucky, because the waiters, seeing their distress, brought out two more platters of hors d'oeuvres. As soon as they sashayed off to the other side of the bar, we ran up and grabbed more and when the debs came back, we had an even taller stack of plates.

Dark looks from the debs. Because we were in sailing clothes? Or because we ate their mini pizzas? Actually, I think it was both. God forbid, sailing clothes in a Yacht Club? The manager of the great Saint Francis Yacht Club came over with complaints from the poor starved little girls, and asked us to leave. We did. I haven't been back since. That's the second time I have had problems there.

All of this was documented in the twice-a-day commentary on Sailing Anarchy.

Racing, ah the racing, there were three boats. We traded boats each race. One fast boat, one slow one, and one in the middle. The fast boat won them all. We only won the regatta due to a great call by Scot Tempesta when we had the dog. We managed a second place with the dog and won.

Thanks Scot! ✆

Ken, Scot, Keith

Life in the Haight

Dane, a high school friend, called me in 1967 and asked if I wanted to go sailing. To San Francisco. On a 26-foot Thunderbird named *Oceola*. From Los Angeles. During what was to become known as the Summer of Love.

A trip of about 400 miles north up the California coast. On a 26-footer with the two kindergarten teachers who owned the boat. We left just when school let out and they constantly drove us nuts by speaking to us like we were 5 year olds.

But being adventurous souls of 16 years of age, the trip sounded like fun. We stopped as often as possible in various harbors to reprovision and to walk on land; generally seeing new places, stopping at remote islands, new harbors (to us) and meeting a lot of very nice people along the way. We listened to Beatles music during this summer of love. *Oceola* made it two thirds of the way to SF to a bay named San Simeon, famed for William Randolph Hurst who built his famous castle on the hill above. The castle is quite elegant with gold leaf pools, gold faucets and sinks. Hurst also had a holy host of animals ranging from aardvarks to zebras roaming freely on the surrounding grounds.

While in San Simeon bay, Dane and I decided to go ashore and check out the small community and send some postcards. Not having a dinghy, we swam. We jumped in and quickly realized that the water was VERY cold, but being 16 and bulletproof, we swam to shore to check out the shops and send postcards to our parents. Knowing what we were in for, the hard part was wading back out into the 48 degree water to swim back to the boat.

Fishing boats would come into the bay to anchor for the night. We waved at them, and they would send over their dingy so we could enjoy each other's good company and fresh fish for dinner. Really good fresh fish!! Albacore!

For three days we attempted to sail north around Point Sur with no luck. It was windy, blowing 35 knots all three days and our little 26 foot plywood *Oceola* just wasn't up to the task. The decision was finally made to turn tail and run back south the 30 miles to Morro Bay where we caught a bus to San Francisco to complete our adventure. San Francisco or bust!

For two 16 year olds, San Francisco in 1967 was Mecca. The hippie movement was in full force and on a lark one evening, Dane and I caught a trolley car to see the city.

The trolley passed by the Fillmore West and when we read the headline bands we just had to get off. Jefferson Airplane, Big Brother and the Holding Company (Janis Joplin), and the Grateful Dead... Jesus, how could you pass that up? There was no limit to the excesses of anything we wanted in there. And it only cost a couple of bucks to get in. The music was good too. I think.

We partied for hours before it ended, but when we left, the trolleys were no longer running. We had to walk the 4 miles back to our hotel.

That's the night I decided that life in San Francisco was ok.

I stayed behind when the others left on the bus back to Morro Bay and the boat. I set up camp in Golden Gate Park with about a thousand others and bought a tarp to sleep under the SF wet. Those of us there had a fine old time, communing in the park and wandering the Haight district doing whatever we felt like doing.

Bands would come to the park and play impromptu free concerts in the afternoons just for the practice. It was just a short walk for the bands from their communal houses in the Haight, and we listened to a lot of their music before it ever hit vinyl.

Most of the music in the park was acoustical as power was not practical, but we neither cared nor noticed. The acid electrical stuff happened on the street in the evenings with power cords run from the houses. Sometimes it was standing room only on Haight Street. Drugs were abundant. Kids were walking around naked and high. This went on till the fall when it started to get cold and everyone went home, or to where ever they wanted to call home.

It was the summer of love under a tarp. My sailing amigos managed to make it back to Los Angeles in one piece and we all caught up a couple of months later to share our adventures (or misadventures) over dinner. They had an exciting sail down the coast with lots of wind behind them, making great time with only a few stops because the teachers were in a hurry to get back to school.

I'm not sure how I got back to LA. It's a fog. But I'll never forget my time under my tarp in the Haight. 🐚

The Holy Smoke Tavern

Each year on Easter weekend, the West Vancouver Yacht Club stages a race called "The Straits Of Georgia" in the waters off Vancouver, British Columbia. Beautiful country, often beneath snow capped mountains. The course varies each year, but is usually in the vicinity of 130 miles long.

My friend Ted Allison and I would make a road trip out of it from Seattle, stopping for two days at the Mount Baker ski area for some snow action. When we finished up our second day of skiing, we would then continue on North to Vancouver, BC, all tired and spent. Taking the back roads north to the border and the steak cookout at West Van Yacht Club, we went through some pretty remote country. Along the way, on an obscure back road, there is an old church that has been converted into a tavern and a biker bar to boot. It's a ramshackle old building and a perfect place for a couple of tired long haired skiers. The Holy Smoke is about half way from the mountain to the yacht club, and a natural watering hole. It has several pool tables, dart boards and foosball tables. We hung out with the nice bikers, had a few beers, played some pool and generally had relaxing fun while winding down from two full days of high speed skiing. We often wound up in many games of pool for money, and we think we broke even. How would we know? It was a great stop on the way to Vancouver and the steak fest.

Then we would have to do the race in all of our ski gear just to try and stay somewhere close to warm in the Canadian cold.

Ted and I eventually learned that the best way to do this race was to do the ski thing at Mount Baker, the Holy Smoke tavern, the steak thing at West Van YC, deliver my sails, and then watch the start from the pier. Then high tail it up to Whistler Mountain for a few more days of well deserved skiing while the sailors slugged it out in 40 knots and snow!

We listened to the radio to find out approximate finish times, then beat it back down to the yacht club for the after race festivities so we could relate sea stories to the people back home. Tanned rested and ready. 🐚

The Gringos Versus the Beaners

During the MEXORC in Manzanillo, Mexico, a spunky and beautiful local woman decided that a spirited contest between the American sailors and the Mexican sailors would promote camaraderie and be fun to boot. An international volleyball match on the sandy beach was chosen as the appropriate arena to determine supremacy of the seas. The game was held on the beach in front of the Las Hadas hotel where Bo Derek lured her admirer in the movie "Ten."

Teams were picked, the net was set up, and off we went for a day of volleyball and fun in the sun and sand. Everything was going well until the beautiful Mexican woman, Suca (Susanna) brought out a case of Tequila. Suca sat on the sidelines and anytime someone missed the ball or a hit, she would run out and grab the culprit's hair, tilt his head back and pour in a healthy shot. She did seem to be more generous with the gringos which didn't do too much for our game. There were lots of crewmembers from other boats on the beach and pretty soon the Tequila ran low so she ran off for more. The game eventually turned into a free for all; the volleyball rules and protocol went out the window. After a bit of this, the game deteriorated to the point where a short cool-down swim and a nap in the sand under an umbrella was necessary. And a little more Tequila too. All in all, it was a successful melding of the two cultures.

Suca went on to marry my amigo Mike Farley. They now live in Colima, Mexico and have two wonderful, grown children. Their daughter Shannon is the spitting image of her mother with long black hair and Mexican features, while Shaun is a towhead blond boy taking after his California dad. It's startling to hear the blond kid speaking rapid fire Spanish!

Shaun has since gone on to win two kite boarding world championships.

Shannon, the baby with the Avocado diaper from another story in this book, didn't marry my son Ryan as Mike and I had hoped, but she lives in San Diego now just a few doors away from him.

Perhaps. ◎

The Hanging Judge Was a Sailor

I once sold a set of sails to a guy who lived 30 miles north of Seattle. He sent in the deposit, we delivered the sails and went out for a test sail. Because he didn't have his checkbook with him and was a known local sailor, I thought I could trust him and said that I would bill him. That was my first mistake. This was back in the innocent days of business.

Back when sailmaking was fun.

After a year with no payment received, I was getting a bit ticked off, naturally. It was about $5,000 and my fledgling business needed the money.

I would call him at 3 a.m. and say "I can't sleep because I can't pay my bills. If I can't sleep, neither should you."

One night, after a Wednesday night race while sitting in a Seattle restaurant, three friends and I decided that this had gone on long enough. We decided to go and repossess the sails off the boat. We drove 30 miles and got to the marina around midnight. We jumped out exuberantly and leapt over the gated marina fence to get to the boat. We had been thinking clearly enough to bring a tire iron to break the lock. So that's what we did. The four of us grabbed MY sails and one extra for good measure, and walked back up the dock to the car.

When we exited the gate with the sails over our shoulders, we saw the police car. Parked right behind our borrowed van. Our van had Idaho license plates and the cops were curious. One of our party of four turned back, dropped his sail and jumped into the 48 degree winter water. We never did find out how he got back to Seattle.

The police had stopped for their dinner doughnuts in the marina and thought it unusual for an Idaho state van to be there in the marina with its side door open and they decided to wait and see why. Well, here we came with our booty. They stepped out of their car and said, "Well boys, what are you doing?" "Well," says I, "I own these sails and am picking them up for repair." "Yea right," they said and made us take the sails back to the boat, which had all the signs of breaking and entering.

There was no way of talking our way out of this one, so we spent the night with the real criminals in the Everett jail. The next morning we called one of our wives to come up and get us. Begrudgingly she did, and we all went for ice creams after our night in the pokey.

On the way home, the three of us criminals decided that buying Lasers would be a good idea. So we did. I lucked into a Laser with the hull number 69069. One of my friends named it *Lickety Split* for me. He said it was a no brainer.

Our court dates were set, and our attorneys were ready. But I had to go and sail in Europe and couldn't make the court date. "No problem," said my attorney, "when will you be back?" I gave her a date and she fixed it. Little did I know I almost wouldn't make it back due to extreme weather in England.

When I returned home, I found that my two fellow captives had been given one year probation and a $600 fine. Not too bad. But my attorney informed me that I had a different judge. And he was the hanging judge, and not lenient at all. This made me a bit nervous to say the least. Would I get jail time?

I went to the judge to plead my case with my attorney and explained the situation; with fear of the hanging judge in my heart.

I needn't have feared; it turned out the judge was a sailor. He knew the person who stole the sails from me. He said that he knew that this person had done this before. This guy was a crook and the judge really couldn't blame me for wanting MY sails back but, never the less, breaking and entering is still against the law. The judge told me that because my other two compatriots had been fined and put on probation, the law said he had to do something. He gave me half the fine and half the probation and said that if it were not for the previous judge's decision, he would have let me off clean.

Lucky for me that the hanging judge was a sailor! ᨧ

The Tallest Mast

The Santa Monica Poor Boys used the California Yacht Club in Marina Del Rey as a base of operations. We sailed dinghies, big boats, and all manner of yachts including RC model boats.

During a Trans Santa Monica bay race, we tried to burn up the 70 foot Blackfin's spinnaker with a lit box of trash. They were following close behind on a rail down reach toward Palos Verdes. We maneuvered directly in front of them, lit the box of trash on fire and carefully set it the water so it would end up right under the foot of their spinnaker. Missed it by this much.

(Hold your arms out wide here.)

After sailing everyone repaired to the bar and had a few. Stories and lies flew, as in every yacht club bar anywhere. Eventually Arnie needed to use the phone. But it wasn't working and he got pissed. Being a fit and strong LA cop, he did the right thing and tore it off the wall and threw it into the ocean. Quarters and all. Perhaps dimes back in the days when sailing was fun. This activity sent the Yacht Club management into a frenzy and they tossed the entire crew out. We of the Santa Monica Poor Boys didn't take kindly to this and decided a late night swim in the yacht club pool would be fun. It was really fun and we had swim contests both on the surface as well as under water. Until the management caught us doing the backstroke naked, checking to see who had the tallest mast. Several of the crew are still not allowed to go there. ᨧ

The USC Sailing Team Goes East

The Kennedy Cup is a very prestigious collegiate regatta hosted by the Naval Academy in Annapolis, Maryland. It was—

and may still be—sailed in the Navy's Luders 44 yawls on the Chesapeake Bay.

In 1969, the USC sailing team somehow finagled an invitation to this prestigious regatta. Being young and spontaneous, part of the crew opted to fly out to the East coast a day early. Upon arrival, they found not much going on, and in the finest USC sailing team tradition, they hit the nearest pub. They then whiled away the hours, chatting up local women and drinking all they could get their young hands on. The five of them, being mostly Irish with names like Hogan, Doran, McClaire, Merickel, and Hambleton, felt right at home in the heavily Irish town and did a fine job of getting themselves fairly hammered. At 2 a.m., they were finally thrown out of one of the many pubs they had abused and made their way down the cobblestone streets to the King George Hotel singing, laughing, belching, farting, and generally shattering the tranquility of the normally quiet upscale neighborhoods along the way. Just as they approached the safety of the front door, the police showed up. Patrol cars from all directions swooped down upon the drunken sailors and in a matter of minutes the "Annapolis 5" were handcuffed and taken to the local pokey. It was there that they spent the night, laughing, giggling, and dozing off in a drunken stupor as they pondered what would befall them.

Come morning, it dawned on them that nobody knew where they were or how they might get out. They were supposed to be at the boat at 10 a.m. that day for a mandatory practice sail. It was a requirement of the regatta. But how could they contact their coach or the other 2 crewmembers who had taken the red eye from L.A. the night before to make bail?

The 2 other crew and the coach, with fine Irish names like MacDonald, Campbell and Meserve, rolled into the King George Hotel in the morning to find their crewmates' rooms empty. No big deal they thought, they must have made their way to the Naval Academy for the mandatory team/skippers meeting, so off they went. At the meeting there was no sign of the Annapolis 5 and concern began to set in with the coach. He wondered where they could they be?

Having sailed and traveled with their mates many times before, MacDonald and Campbell had a pretty good idea. Let's try the local jail they suggested to the coach. So off they went and sure enough, there were the Annapolis 5. Hung-over, sleepless, bleary eyed and bedraggled, but ready to go sailing if they could only get out of jail.

The coach asked the officer at the desk when they could be released and were told that they would be held until court proceedings could take place. Bad news. The mandatory practice race the first day required the entire team be onboard its assigned boat at the Naval academy in two hours.

The coach and the two free crewmen scrambled to contact the local presiding judge and woke him up at home. They pleaded their case and convinced him to come to court early and grant the offenders a hearing in his personal chambers. The disheveled team members, fresh from their night in jail, were brought in wearing chains, led by the arresting officer.

Good news, the judge was a USC graduate and of Irish decent as well. He looked over and asked the officer what had the boys done? "Aw, they was just skylarkin 'n stuff. You know, singing shanteys and generally makin' a drunken nuisance of themselves."

The judge peered over his glasses at the boys, looked down at the fine Irish names-Hogan, McClaire, Doran, Merickel, MacDonald, Campbell and, struggling to keep a straight face, severely scolded the "boys" for their "shenanigans" and told them in no uncertain terms that if he ever saw them again, he wouldn't be so kind. Now go out and win this regatta! Which they did in fine fashion, albeit a bit hung over. 🦪

Turning is for Sissies

One winter, a group of us went on a ski trip to Sun Valley and asked an old buddy, Ken Gussian from L.A. along. "Sure," he said, "but I am not that good a skier." "No problem," said we, "Many of the runs are easy and well groomed and you can learn as you go."

Well, nobody taught him how to turn and Ken being a go-for-it-kind of guy thought you just went straight down. The run we were on had a gentle turn in the middle of it that Ken failed to negotiate. He went straight off a bump into the trees at a high rate of speed. We found him hanging upside down in a tree, suspended by his skis.

We skied over to him and asked him why he didn't make the turn? Upside down he looked at us and said with a smile, "Turning is for sissies." We laughed and replied, "Hanging upside down from a tree is not all that a good of a look either." So we taught him how to turn. ⚅

Welcome to Japan

The Japan Cup is sailed out of Muira, a small town about 70 miles south of Tokyo. I was recruited by our Japanese sail loft owner, Mikio Tokano, to come over and steer a 41 foot boat with his sails and I could bring two other American sailors with me.

I asked Norman and Mikey to be my accomplices. I should have known better. I had never been to Japan before and neither had they, but it seemed like a big adventure.

I asked Mikio how much money I needed to bring, and he said, "Money? For what?" "What if I want to buy the owner a drink?" Mikio said, "Oh my god, don't offer that, it'll cause him to lose face." "Ok what if I want film?" "Go to the front desk and put it on your bill." Ok, I get it.

The drive from Tokyo to Miura was slow due to traffic, but uneventful. Mikio needed to stop by his sail loft so he could check up on the day's events. We entered the loft and, after removing our shoes and donning slippers, we were informed that lunch was being served in our honor. Nice. They have a beautiful little area out back, in a lovely Japanese (duh) garden, with a traditional Japanese table set down low. We were more than just a little tired and cramped after flying from San Francisco to Japan, but the show must go on!

After flying economy class in the VERY small seats that cater to the usual Japanese clientele, we were hard pressed to scrunch down with our legs crossed on the floor, but we did it with a smile out of respect for our host. Also because there was a cold beer at each of our places and lovely Japanese girls in traditional kimonos serving. Nice touch.

Mikio introduced us to his workers at the sail loft, whose names we had no chance of properly pronouncing, let along remembering later. Then we were introduced to the owner of the boat we'd be sailing, who had graciously sponsored this welcome luncheon.

All was going along swimmingly because we spoke no Japanese, only Mikio spoke English, and we all like beer, Saki, miso soup, and bits of sashimi. Things began to go awry when Norman spied a fish eye in his first course of soup. I asked Mikio what was up with this, but he just laughed and said that it was a traditional Japanese delicacy, and that out of respect for the boat owner, Norman should eat it and smile! (Have some more beer first). Norman was more than a little apprehensive about this, especially with Mikio laughing. Mike and I were apprehensive too, as our own "eyes" had not seen us yet. Mikey and I did eventually come to our own moment of international crossroads but we had to go for it; somewhat like eating a worm on one of those reality shows.

They weren't too bad. A bit crunchy, "tastes like chicken" but we held to the notion that the locals had been eating fish eyeballs for centuries and they were healthy... Or were they? They were STILL smiling and laughing at us...

After a lovely lunch, we were taken to our digs for the week, a beautiful old hotel right on the water. There weren't any other buildings within a quarter of a mile, but there was a rack of about 30 Lasers behind the pool! The pool, however, was black with algae, and there were very few other guests.

But just outside our rooms was a BEER MACHINE. 200 Yen and you got a very large Japanese beer! Paradise with an ocean view. Nice.

Our first race in the Japan Cup was a thing of beauty. One that writers write about, and one we would have won except for the OCS. Norman remarked that it's a sad state of affairs when the sailing has to get in the way of all the fun.

The next day was the long distance race. It was 300 miles around a volcano, with a few random volcanic islands thrown in for fun. The start was just plain light and not much fun, but it gradually built to about 15 knots making a nice spinnaker run for the fleet. We were tooling along nicely when one of the Japanese crew yelped. Apparently he had dropped his wallet over the side. I offered the owner a "wallet overboard drill" but was told no in no uncertain terms. If the crewman was dumb enough to have his wallet in his pocket, it was his problem.

In the afternoon, the wind worked its way around forward and we were perched on the rail. Lunch. Have you ever eaten a Cup O' Soup with chop sticks (hashi) upwind in 20 knots? The gringos almost starved on this race. Rice-Fish-Rice-Tea was the fare.

Near the end of the race, while jib reaching on starboard at 4 a.m. toward the finish some 25 miles off, Norman, my tactician, whispered to me to drive faster. I said, "I'm trying to drive the best I can." He replied, "You have to drive faster." "Why?" "Look behind you." I turned around and there was a giant waterspout 100 yards behind us. Holy shit!

I willed the boat on and it missed us by a couple of hundred yards.

After finishing at 7:30 a.m. or so, we stopped at a local eatery for breakfast before going back to the hotel. Norman and Mike ordered the western style breakfast of bacon and eggs. I thought to myself, "when in Rome" and ordered the Japanese breakfast which consisted of a fish along with a number of unrecognizable items. After a hearty meal of fish and fish soup, Mikio asked if we would like to sample a special Japanese delicacy. After our first experience with a special Japanese delicacy of fish eyes, I was a little reluctant but in the spirit of adventure, agreed. So he ordered three orders of Nato. We should have known that three orders indicated something special for a ten man crew.

Nato is fermented beans with a sauce over which you break a raw egg. You then stir the whole mess up with your hashi until it becomes a sticky, gloopy glob of stuff that sticks to your sticks like peanut butter. And boy does it taste like fermented beans. Once again Mikio and his boys were rolling in the aisles over this. RF'd again by the locals.

When Mikio dropped us off at our hotel, he told us dinner was to be at a nice sushi bar where we would meet up with the rest of the crew. Oh boy, more fish eyes! And the following day was a whole day off to boot. We planned to go check out some lasers and go sailing! The hotel was alive with teenage boys and girls who had a bunch of 420's in the water, but few Lasers. Lucky day for us, we might borrow three! So we sauntered up to the person sitting behind the desk with many clipboards, and explained that we were visiting from America and were sailing in the Japan Cup. This really set off a frenzy. Japan Cup, Japan Cup! The news went through the crowd like wildfire, and soon we were surrounded by a mob of orange lifejackets.

Understand that this was mostly accomplished with sign language. We spoke no Japanese, and for the most part they spoke no English. Eventually a Japanese student who spoke some English eagerly translated answers to their many questions about the race, and sailing in the U.S. We finally got around to the issue of us borrowing three Lasers. No, we were told, No, not possible! No way. After all that? We had to console ourselves with a few beers from the machine and watch them sail in 12 knots on a beautiful bright sunny day. Oh well.

That evening, Mikio picked us up for dinner, which was quite nice and went smoothly, with only minor food faux pas, after which our owner excused himself early for the night. We learned later that this was so the crew could go out on their own to show the Americans around and have some fun. Once our owner had left, Mikio asked us if we would like to visit a nice quiet bar near his house for a drink. Why, of course we would. He took us into this dark bar room with very few customers. The hostess came up to our host and gave him an un-sisterly hug and bid us all to sit down. Mikio asks the Americans what we would like to drink and we each request a gin and tonic. Simple, we thought, until after two minutes of rapid fire local speak she ran out of the bar and returned a few minutes later with a bottle of gin and set it down on the table. Mikio looked at her with a smirk and a pinch and some more rapid fire Japanese until she ran out again for the tonic she forgot.

Her job for the whole night was to make sure our glasses didn't get more than a half inch down from the top. The rest of the Japanese crew was drinking Bourbon, and did themselves proud. Then the Karaoke started. Crap.

I didn't know I couldn't sing until that night. Friends never tell you these things. I didn't know the words to Yesterday either. (Even with the words on the screen). Norman can't sing either, and proved it by trying to sing Yesterday. With two bottles of bourbon gone and most of the gin, it eventually became time to exit. But not before a few more friendly hugs. Upon hitting the street we Americans turned away from the smiling hostess, grabbed our pants and began to tug at our belts. The Japanese could see what was coming and in the spirit of an international bonding experience of sailors, they had their pants down before we did. We all were singing Yesterday in different languages as we marched down the narrow street toward the car with our pants at our ankles.

The car. This next part is a story about the car. And the car had a driver. Well, we had all had a few, except for the driver, and were warm as it was a warm night so the two sunroofs of the car were open. There was one over the front seat and one over the back seat. Our dear friend Mike decided that it was a little crowded in the back seat and it would only be fitting and right to move to the front seat. Via the two sunroofs. So there we were tooling down a very narrow, very dark road. It was very late (thank goodness) and we were going quite fast. Did you know that in Japan they drive on the left hand side of the road and the driver sits on the right? Neither did Mikey. He climbed out the rear sunroof, across the top of the car to the forward sunroof and made a crash landing on the driver's lap nearly causing a major high speed crash.

We lived, but were not invited back to Japan for many years. 🐌

Almost Sinking an Islander 40

For the Three Tree Point rock race out of the Corinthian Yacht Club in Seattle, my customer John, asked me to steer his Doug Peterson designed Islander 40, *Quicksilver*.

Sure, why not says I. His daughter Debbie was working for me in the sail loft, and is a good sailor. She was going along as well. He had the whole crew set up but had suddenly been sent out of town on business and asked me to drive the boat in his absence.

The race goes south from Seattle to Des Moines (WA) and back. A windward leeward course of about 35 miles. This year it was really windy, starting out medium at around fifteen knots, but building to the mid thirties on the beat to the turning mark. Half way up the beat we were in the #4 Genoa with a double reef in the main. It was really blowing, and the wind was against the tide.

Just before the mark, Johns boat partner asked me tentatively if I was going to set a spinnaker after the mark. Let's wait and see I suggested, to his dismay.

We had sailed a great beat, and gotten a few breaks, to round second just a couple boat lengths behind a C&C 44, and ahead of several larger boats.

I asked the crew to keep an eye on the 44 and tell me if they were getting ready to set a spinnaker. Sure enough, they were. "Ah shit," we all said. Put the 1.5 oz up on the foredeck, and get it ready. They set a small storm spinnaker, and we all groaned. We only had a full size sail, and they had thrown down the gauntlet. "Let's go for it," I said, to the great dismay of the boat partner.

We managed to hang on for 25 minutes or so, in 40 knots of cold wind, plaining away from the C&C 44, and having a ball too! Hooray, we're doing great! Till the inevitable caught up with us.

The wind was hovering around 40K, against a flood tide, and throwing up a large chop. We were having a bit of a hard time getting through it with this old I.O.R. design, but so far so good. Until a bigger bit of chop came along that the boat wasn't up to. The bow dove into the wave and slowed down with water over the deck past the mast and coming into the cockpit. On a forty foot cruising boat, In surfing we call this pearling.

The boat was still going straight, and eventually stopped and fell over on its side. Debbie pointed out the fore hatch as it floated by. Little did we know the damage that was being done to the forepeak with no fore hatch, but we were too concerned with lying flat on our side and making sure we were all ok.

Debbie had been standing behind me, and was pressed hard up against me, and the weight of the two of us, and the rapid deceleration, bent the wheel.

The first thing you do in a time like this is blow the spinnaker halyard to get yourself upright.

This didn't work as the spinnaker was wrapped around the masthead. Shit. We lay flapping on our side unable to get the boat back up, while the shore loomed a mile away. And the boat was full of water to boot. It took us 20 minutes to get her back on her feet and sailing toward the finish. There was two feet of water from the missing fore hatch, and we bailed all the way to the finish. We managed to get a second place finish after lying down for 30 Minutes.

At the dock the crew finished the bailing, fitted some plywood to cover the fore hatch for the rain, and generally recovered from the experience. Shock and awe! The forepeak was fire hosed, blowing out joinery, bunks, and drawers. We were still bailing two hours later.

At Corinthian Y.C. later, we had the reverse comments. Normally you go in telling tales of your adventures on the race course, and your friends call bullshit. We went in and our racer friends came up to saying "wow, I can't believe what happened to you guys!" Apparently, most of the trailing edge of the keel was visible, the propeller, and the rudder were sky high!

We nonchalantly said "aw, it was nothing, just another day on the water."

We all went home after warming up, thinking of our near disaster.

Debbie had to go home and talk with her dad, who had called to hear of the results. So she told him what had happened in an off hand way.

He called back a few minutes later with a "what happened?"

The boat was fine, but we weren't. &

Ahh, Fred and the Night Visitor

Fred Olson and Davey (aka Dr. Kato) liked to row out in the night to the middle of Lake Union in Seattle with some "warming fluids" where they would drink several bottles of wine and Davey would play his concertina. They rowed around the lake singing "Yo Ho Ho" into the wee hours of the morning.

One morning around 2 a.m., they ran out of wine and decided to row over to my houseboat. They knew that I had several cases of South African wine I had just brought back from Cape Town. In my sleep I heard them row down our waterway and heard Davey say, "Let's get some of Keith's really good South African wine" as the concertina continued to play. Yo Ho Ho!

I leaped out of bed and locked all the doors (we never had a key hidden outside because we never locked the doors!) and listened as they tried in vain to get in the back sliding glass door, then the front door. Failing to gain entry, they woke up the neighbors by talking loudly about going through the bathroom skylight. I went into the bathroom, which was on the water side of the house, and opened the window to look out at them. There, hanging from my rain gutter was Dr Kato, laughing and giggling while Fred tried to boost him up to the roof. My J-24 was tied up behind the house and when the rain gutter broke, down went Kato right between the boat and the dock into the 48 degree water. It's been said that god protects drunks and fools, and in this case it's true because Kato hit neither his head nor chin on his way down. Fred fell laughing into my bathroom window, breaking it.

By the time Fred and I got Kato out of the water, my wife had a hot bath waiting; she had been through this drill before. We got the chill off of him before calling his wife to come and get him, (he lived on another houseboat down the street). She told us it served him right and to let him walk home. It was about a mile and he had no dry clothes so it fell upon me to drive the two of them home to angry wives. Singing Yo Ho Ho and a bottle of South African wine all the way!

Similar nocturnal visits were not uncommon, but this was the first time they had come up with the brilliant idea of hanging from the roof. They seemed to learn their lesson about it not being a great idea, and that never happened again.

This was a special occasion. 🐚

Beach Blanket Bingo

One year, some of our Taxi Dancer crew went on a day tour of the Mexican Rivera during a MexORC. We visited Barra Da Navidad, Mulahae, and a few others, with a last stop in the beautiful little hamlet of Carayes.

There is a fancy hotel there on the beach with a beautiful pool where they pour huge Margaritas with copious quantities of Tequila. I suppose the lack of clientele may have something to do with this.

We sent Davey for another pitcher, and while he was waiting, one of the crew walked up behind him and pantsed him in front of all the other guests. He calmly stood there with his junk hanging out while the bartender mixed the drinks. He then pulled his pants up so he could walk over to the lounge chairs where we were sitting.

After finishing off the pitcher, we noticed Mike and Nancy were missing. We looked around and they were nowhere to be found. Oh well, we thought, they'll turn up.

A short time later, Mike came back with a Mount Gay hat over his privates and a sheepish look on his face. It seems that they had snuck over to the next cove for some extracurricular activities and while they were getting busy, a wave had come in and washed their clothes away. We all had a good laugh over this and loaned them our beach towels so he could go back and look for their clothes. After what seemed an extra long time, they wandered back still wrapped up in our towels looking flushed. We gave them a boisterous round of applause and to this day we haven't let them forget it.

On the ride back to Manzanillo, one of the girls got a little frisky and moved her man to the back of the VW bus, slipped her skirt up, pulled her panties down, slipped his shorts down and they made love all the way home in the bouncy VW bus. They might have gone unnoticed till she started making moaning sounds.

In the end, we gave them a standing ovation too! ◎

Funnelating the Police Boat

One year before the Congressional Cup at Long Beach Yacht Club, a friend and I found my funnelator in the back of my VW bus. For those of you who aren't familiar with this, a funnelator is a very powerful water balloon launcher.

Off to the store for balloons we went...

After filling them up, we set up on Con Cup row and lobbed a few balloons at passing boats, and making the occasional strike. It wasn't too long before the police boat motored by looking for our launch pad but they couldn't see us. We had almost unbelievable range and could fire from the head of the dock. So there they were, sitting ducks, so we lobbed one into them, then another, then another. It was like stirring up a hornets nest. It didn't take long before we heard sirens from police cars. We dropped the funnelator and ran like hell across the street where we leapt the fence of a well known sailing writer to hide in his back yard to wait it out. They patrolled around for hours while we hid. They actually looked over the fence once, but we were well hidden.

Finally after several hours we were able to escape to my car, parked at Long Beach Yacht Club and putter away, looking completely innocent.

After all, it was just water.

Damn, I lost a great funnelator too! ⊗

Sailing on a Shoestring

Almost every year one of my crew and I would drive the 800 mile trip from Seattle to San Francisco towing my Olson 30 Wildfire for the Leukemia Cup.

The regatta was usually held in May on the city front near Saint Francis Yacht Club. After driving the boat down, we would leave the boat in SF for the summer. The schedule each year was the same: we left Seattle at 6:00 a.m. in order to get to Mike Ellis's (my boat partner) log cabin 8 miles up a dirt road in Gold Hill, Oregon, in order to arrive in time for some gold panning. Then one of Glenda's fabulous steak dinners, complete with all manner of fresh picked vegetables.

Michael and Glenda are farmers and have crops. Enough to keep their family in fruit and vegetables for the year: corn, cabbage, carrots, tomatoes, green beans, pumpkins, spinach, artichokes, melons, zucchini and more. They also have an orchard with pear, apple, cherry and plum trees.

They also have blue jays and crows, both of whom also loved to eat their crops. Their winter food.

When we arrived around 4 p.m., Mike usually had his 22 caliber rifle out. Cleaned and loaded. After we were cleaned and loaded, he would point out where the blue jays were hiding and instruct us to "go get 'em." No problem for us city boys. Picking a blue jay off a tree branch at 40 paces is dead easy. Glenda never liked the birds but having dead ones hanging from her clothes line with clothes pins was a bit unsettling for her.

He also had an ongoing problem with critters: deer, raccoons and skunks mostly. When we arrived with Wildfire in tow in the afternoon, he would ask us for help with the critter problem, too.

One particular night after a delicious steak dinner, a coon got into a corrugated drain pipe that had not yet been laid into the ground. We heard him scrambling around outside and thought we could catch him. We grabbed a pillow case and went outside. Mike held the pillowcase over one end to capture the coon, while I raised the other end in the hope we could shake him out. Imagine a raccoon spread eagled inside of a corrugated pipe.

I often wonder now what we would do with him if we had caught him. Or, worse, what he would do to us.

There is nothing quite as nasty as an agitated raccoon. In the long run, we were lucky that he wouldn't shake out of the pipe.

The next morning we took off around 4 a.m. for the second half of the trip over the Siskiyous and down to San Francisco arriving about noon to do a rig up and boat launch.

The problem with a thousand mile drive is that things shake loose. One time we pulled into San Francisco with a missing outhaul shackle. I had to take the stainless steel fore guy shackle off the pole bridle and use it as a replacement outhaul part, then use a shoelace to lash the block to the pole bridal as a replacement of the shackle.

It was always part of our practices to tune the rig mid-day Friday with a short crew and pickups off the dock, then come back in around 2:30 to pick up the balance of the crew who had just flown in from Seattle. When everyone was settled, we took off for a "Frisco wake up call." This meant taking the lily white Seattle sailors out for a spin in the big breeze of the bay. Our normal practice was to beat across to the North Tower of the Golden Gate Bridge. One particular time it was blowing well over 30 knots. The whole crew was there and my wife came along for the ride. We sailed into the lee of the yellow bluff cliffs and rigged up Patches, our old practice spinnaker, for the reach back to the yacht club. The Seattle guys looked at me and saying something like, It's really windy out there, are you sure? To which I replied, are you going to hair out on me tomorrow when we're racing? If you are, go home tonight.

It was a hair-raising broad reach back to the yacht club. Going as fast as an Olson 30 will go. The main was flapping, crew hiking way aft with two hiking off the transom. It was fine...until the red ferry went by throwing up a big wake. Right in front of Saint Francis YC.

Now I know you have all heard crews bragging about spreaders in the water.

After we leapt over the first wave and hit bottom, the shoelace on the forguy broke, the pole skied and we went down with a smack. So hard my boots, which were not being worn at the time, were thrown from the cockpit. Thankfully, most of the crew were hiked and able to hang on to lifelines or a stanchion. I was sitting legs in and tossed into the leeward lifelines and the water. The damn boat tried to buck me off in retaliation for all the abuse I'd given it in San Francisco over the years.

The upshot was that the mast hit the water so fast and so hard that Patches was washed through between the cap shrouds, top spreader and mast and filled with water like a giant balloon. Pinned by the weight of the water-filled spinnaker at the top of the mast, we were down for about four minutes with water lapping up toward the hatch. The only thing to do was have our youngest foredeck mountain climber walk up the mast while holding on to the shrouds. I cautioned him that when he got the mess untangled, it would be wise for him to run down the rig as fast as possible. So there he was, straddling the mast above the top spreader trying to get the mess cleared while we were fumbling around for the hatch board to keep the water from splashing into the cabin.

We did manage to get the mess straightened out and the comments on the dock from other practicing boats were "Are you guys ok?" Of course we were. Any landing you can walk away from... And we won the regatta to boot!!

We left a pretty good sized divot on the bay though. Been done before I'm sure... And Patches made it through unscathed as well!!

My wife looked at me with scorn and asked, "Is this what you consider fun?" "Damn, I lost a good boot," was all I said. Because, yes, I do it for fun. ✆

Wildfire in SF

Upside Down in the Southern Ocean

In 1973, I was invited to sail on *Sayula II* for the first Whitbread Round the World race. We were at 61 degrees south, about 1250 miles southwest of Perth, Australia. It was blowing 60 knots, with higher gusts with similar conditions for the prior three days.

The main was down and lashed to the boom and we were sailing with just a storm jib and storm staysail up. Even with that small amount of sail up, we were still just holding on.

Then came the bad news. Over the radio, we heard that Paul Waterhouse had been lost overboard from Tauranga, a Swan 55, and that Jean Pierre Millet was lost from 33 Export and they had decided to proceed to Perth.

In these conditions we split our watches of four in half and let one half sit below in their gear, ready in case they were needed on deck. There wasn't much to do on deck in these conditions but get cold and wet.

We did make snowmen and snow angels one day just for fun.

One day in November, the day after Thanksgiving, I was off watch cleaning my camera on the starboard lower main salon bunk when the skylight overhead went black and the boat lurched. We were picked up by a giant whitecap and tossed down a big wave landing on its starboard cabin side. Two 6 millimeter ports were broken out. Imagine putting a model boat in the surf at the beach. It was like that. I was tossed up into the upper bunk, then the floorboards fell on top of me, pinning me in. The water started filling up the corner I was trapped in. Butch was on the port side and fell down after the floorboards. As the boat slowly righted itself, he pulled the boards off me and pulled me out of the water. I can still remember how cold that water was!

Several of the crew were injured and unable to help, but the rest of us bailed for three hours before we realized that we weren't going to sink. The bilge pumps were plugged with balloons from the Thanksgiving party the Mexicans had thrown for the Americans. We uninjured crew gave the injured guys the bunks and we slept on the cabin floor on newspapers.

I learned then that no bilge pump can match frightened sailors bailing! 🐚

How to **Get a Ride in the**
"Round the World Race"

I began my sailmaking career at the age of nineteen while living in a Volkswagen bus. I lived and loved in this bus for three years, often parking in the lot at Sails by Watts at night and, after surfing, going off to El Camino College in the early am for some volleyball, and a shower.

When I was 22, I did a long sailboat race, a very long sailboat race.

At work in the sail loft one day while hand working a ring into the clew of a Swan 65 main, I asked my longtime sailing pal Bill Petersen why all these sails for a Mexican boat are being shipped to Finland. He told me that this crazy Mexican guy was going to do the first Whitbread Round The World Race, and in an offhand way, he said"why don't you call him up and go along?" Well now, I had never been further away from home than Mexico, having raced in some Taco Derby's, but the thought flashed before me of all the fun places where a kid of 22 years could get into trouble. So, on this dare, I called them. I called Irv Loube who was the US organizer for Ramon Carlin, the owner of the Swan 65. I told him I was currently building his sails, I had some good sailing references, and could I go on the race? Half an hour later I was a member of the crew for the First Whitbread Round the World Race in 1973. I had no idea what I was in for, but I was and still am not timid about adventure.

All I could see was England, Cape Town, Sydney, and Rio De Janeiro.

I had no inkling of the 44 day passage from the UK to Cape town What it would be like or what it could do to you. I was only thinking of ports and adventure. During Transpac 1973 it began to dawn on me when 2/3 of the way across the Pacific, I started to go a bit stir crazy. My buds began to chide me about how short Transpac was compared to the WTWR. No help from your friends is there, so I resorted to pranks as noted elsewhere in this book to pass the time. We did finally make it to Hawaii where I was able to spend 3 days before flying home to prepare for my big adventure.

I flew home, sold my beloved VW bus, and took off for England. A stranger in a strange land I was. I hunted for two days for the boat in the south of England. From Portsmouth to Lymington. From Ryde to Cowes, sleeping in parking lots, I looked and looked, before finally hearing that the boat was on the Hamble River. I took a ferry back across the Solent and began to walk the three miles to the Hamble, where I hoped the boat would be.

Did I mention that my hair was down below my shoulders and I had a large moustache? It wasn't easy to get rides being a Southern California hippie, but along came a car with people hanging out of the windows, whooping and yelling in Spanish. They skidded to a stop by me and said, "you must be Keith". Boy was I relieved to not be walking any further! I threw my bags in and jumped in. We all introduced ourselves, went off to the pub, and had a fine English dinner. I think they might have been a little taken aback by the tired, dirty, longhair they had picked up, but after a few pints at the pub, all was well and the rest is history. We all became a family, something I think is lacking in racing these days. Ramon Carlin is still to this day, a second father to me. *Sayula II* won the very first fully crewed race around the planet, of which I am proud to have had a part in. There will be lots of *Sayula II* stories throughout this book, but this is about a car trip I was an unwilling part of in San Francisco.

During the RTWR, both the BBC and the ITV of England made movies. They handed some of us movie cameras and film and said "shoot at will" Well we all did, and the some of the results were included in a rather fun film called "The Greatest Race". I think the ITV's movie was "The Great Adventure"

Upon my return to California, I went to see if I could get my old sailmaking job back. Stunningly, the answer was NO. But, due to my newfound fame from the WTWR, I could become a salesman!! My brother Ed Lorence was a salesman there and I had always wanted to rise to the prominence of that position!! Happy day!! Anyway, one of my jobs would be to tour around Southern California, showing the movie, giving talks, answering questions, and generally promoting Sails By Watts. One of the Gigs involved going to St Francis Yacht Club, and doing the same. Well, this was too much of a boondoggle for the owner of the company Burke Sawyer, head of sales Ed Lorence and my best bud Billy Petersen to pass up.

So there we all are at the Saint Francis YC after the presentation is over, with nothing to do in San Francisco.

Burke decides it's time to go over to North Beach and the Buena Vista cafe for an Irish coffee. We did have a fairly good size car for the four of us, Thankfully. To get to North beach, one has several options. Past the navy base, past Ghiradellies, or up and over the top of the hill and down Lombard, the crookedest street in the world.

I had never been down Lombard before, and had no idea what Burke had in mind, but going up the hill from the West we were gaining speed. I remember my brother saying "oh no, you're not going to do this!" And buckling his seat belt.

We cleared the pavement at the top in the best Clint Eastwood style, cleared the first bank of planters, surrounded by a shower of sparks, and screaming locals, and went straight down Lombard. At the bottom, Burke did a nice hand brake turn so we all could look back up at the swath of destruction straight down Lombard. I believe that it had never been done before, and hasn't been done since.

They have since built up the planter box curbs, making it even more of a challenge for someone to top Burke's run. 🐚

Sayula II

Rental car at the airport

After a sailmaking company meeting, 4 of us had an 80 mile drive to the airport in Atlanta, so naturally we had to stop for some beers. A twelve pack of course, as it's a long drive.

Upon arrival, we parked at the sidewalk to walk in and check the flight information. This happened to be right next to a bar, so 4 Gin and tonics seemed right. 4 became 8, and then it was time for our plane, so off we go.

Just as the plane was taking off, the owner of our franchise, whom shall remain nameless, said "oh shit, the rental car" It was left with the engine running at the curb. Never found out what happened to it, but it had to be good, and expensive. 🐚

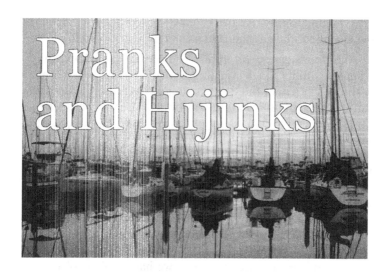

Skinny Dipping Ipanima Beach

While in downtown Rio De Janiro, one of the American sailors came across an American stewardess. He asked her where they were staying and if he could visit her at the hotel. She would not tell him where they were staying, rules you know. So he asked if she wanted to go for a sail on his large yacht on one of their days off, and if the rest of her flight crew wanted to join, they could meet us at the Yacht Club De Rio De Janiro at noon.

The next day noon came around, and a cab with 4 lovely young girls looking for a fun day sail while on their layover in Rio. Cool! All went well, and it was a beautiful sail around the harbor in Rio. Half naked American girls who just wanted to go wild on their off days. Girls gone wild! They sailed with us for two days and spent the nights with us on the boat.

One evening one of the girls said "we are leaving tomorrow- back to New York. But can we send the next flight crew down for a 'sail'?" But of course!!

Two days later at noon, after a day of recuperation, another group of off duty stews showed up at the Yacht club.

After talking to the first group, they wanted to go sailing and swimming for the day too, and a few days after as well.

After four weeks of rotation, one group decided that skinny dipping Ipanima beach at midnight could be fun. Off we went to the beach where the 8 of us stripped off our clothes and jumped into the 80' water. Swimming, laughing and generally having a great time. Doing what you do when you become naked. Later, when it was time to go ashore, we found the federalies holding up the ladies panties on the end of their AK 47's. The naked male sailors came ashore first, and in broken Portuguese and sign language said "give the girls their clothes". The bashful boys did, so the girls could get out of the water with their dignity semi intact. They then took us to a holding cell and locked the door. After an hour or two, one of the brighter bulbs on the Christmas tree said "let's empty our pockets and see how much money we have". We pooled our money and he then knocked on the door and showed the feds a handful of Cruseros, whereupon we were released and had to walk home at 4 AM.

What a night was had by all, and one that will not be forgotten soon. 🐚

Hail Lucinda!

Some years ago, David Jones, a good friend of mine, returned from Haiti and presented me with a voodoo doll. An anatomically correct female voodoo doll! He explained how she worked her magic in great detail.

First, you write the name of whom you wish to hex on a blank piece of white paper. (I have only once used a person's name, usually just a boat). Then wrap her and the paper in a white sheet, shirt, or whatever, and chant the hexee's name three times. Then put her in a dark place and watch the fireworks. Naturally I was a somewhat dubious about this, and waited several years before putting her to the test. I named her Lucinda.

Lucinda's first task was during the J 35 North Americans on San Francisco bay in 1987. We were in second place going into the last day, and for whatever reason, I had brought her along with me to San Francisco. Unbeknownst to the crew, I performed the ritual that morning with my room mate, chanting the name of the boat I wanted to hex three times, and left her in a closet in our hotel.

There were two races that last day, and in the second race, first beat with the regatta on the line, the hexee's jib car blew up. They were able to find another car and continue sailing, till the Jib halyard broke. Using a second halyard, they were still somewhat close, but then the jib luff tape jammed in the pre feeder at the leeward mark. If this wasn't enough to remove them from the hunt, they fouled another boat on the last beat, and were DSQ'd.

I think she was pissed at them because she had to spend a day in a closet!

Hail Lucinda!

That's when I became a believer in witchcraft.

In a major Southern California regatta, the Sir Thomas Lipton Cup, Yacht Clubs from all over the southern California send their best. The team I was coaching, SDYC, was in third place beginning the last day. On a hunch on the way out to the start, I transferred from the coach boat to the race boat with my duffel bag and requested a crew meeting. I spoke a little about tactics and strategy, and crew work, (which was already very good).

This was all a lead up to Lucinda. When I broke out this voodoo stuff, they were wondering if I was nuts... I opened my bag and brought out Lucinda.

They all laughed, but went along with the kooky old guy. We did the whole routine. I had Chris Snow, the skipper write the name of the boats they needed to beat, wrap her up, and then the whole crew chanted the boat names three times.

In a miraculous comeback, and I mean from WAY back, the SDYC team pulled it out in the last race. The other two teams had total meltdowns, and we won! Our team now believes in voodoo. The e mails flew on Monday morning.

Hail Lucinda!

The only time I ever used her with a person's name was after he totally pissed me off by trying to tell me how to trim a sail while I was already in the process of doing exactly what he was yelling at me to do. How many times do you have to hear this before you turn around and say "shut up" I am already doing it! Just watch me turn the traveler handle! Some people get so twisted up in their own self importance that they think they know everything and lose sight of their main job as tactician. That might be keeping a calm demeanor and a sense of composure. These are the same people who yell at the bow people, as if that will help. We have all been there and seen that. So I turned to Lucinda for help. Not to injure, but to heap lots of bad luck upon him.

Over the course of several months, he became responsible for a large boat program to collapse; he was flicked from another major program. Shortly thereafter, his services on another prominent boat were deemed unnecessary.

He has rebounded somewhat lately since I let Lucinda out of the white shirt.

But pay back is a bitch.

Hail Lucinda!

She has been called upon to help several times and comes through 80% of the time.

Don't mess with Lucinda.

Or me... 🐚

74

How to Rustle a Horse in the City
or Mr. Ed Goes Yachting

Everyone's good friend Tim Lynch, well known surfer and sailor, had a life size plastic horse in the back forty on Point Loma, San Diego.

He asked me to sail with him on his Etchells 22 in the SDYC opening day race, and did I have anyone who could come with us? Well, I said, my sister in law Dee Dee is in town, and had crewed for us the year before on the Schock 35, but had very little experience. (This would be her second race ever). Tim said in his easy going way "it'll all be ok".

Doing the bow on an Etchells 22 was a bit of a reach for a girley girl from Hull, Massachusetts, but she pulled it off though-with a bit of help from her friends.

Opening day is a reverse start race with around 35 boats, and thru smoke and mirrors, we managed to win. Vince Brun on his Melges 24 came close, but he got stuck behind an incoming freighter. After the race, Tim being Tim, thought that it would be fun to park the boat on the YC guest dock in front of the bar for the night.

Later in the evening, a friend and I decided that the only fitting and right thing to do would be to rustle Tim's horse and place him on the boat. So off we went at ten PM to rustle a full size plastic horse.

When we arrived at the corral (back yard) to abscond with said horse, Tim's son was playing computer games while Tim was watching TV. We had to go around back to do the dirty deed without them seeing us.

Snaring the horse was easy, as he was pretty tame, but tying him down to the top of the Subaru with sail ties was a bit of work. As we were driving away laughing, a thought came across. It's midnight, we've had a couple of drinks, and we have a horse tied to the roof... We are horse thieves and they hang them,.. Don't they?... What would we say to a policeman?? Sorry sir, but we hit this horse on the way home from the valley and will take him to the glue factory tomorrow? Luckily for us, we made it without a hitch from the police, but many sideways glances, especially from the guards at SDYC.

We took Mr. Ed down to the boat, set him up on the foredeck tying his mane to the forestay and tail to the spinnaker pole car, and left him for the night. The next morning at 5 AM I donned my wetsuit, woke up Dee Dee, and we walked on up to the club for a cup of coffee.

After our coffee, I jumped on the boat, pushed it off the dock towards the center channel, and dropped the anchor 100 feet from the club, jumped in the water and swam back to the front deck.

Looking around, I realized that the opening day party from the night before had left a lot of balloons around.

Well, of course Tim's boat needed balloons!! I grabbed about ten, swam out to the boat and, in a festive way, decorated the boat and swam back to my still warm coffee. Watching the startled faces of the early morning coffee klatch.

I can still recall J 24 national champion Chris Snow walking down the dock with his kids asking him "dad, is that a real horse?" When they would look away Chris would say "look-he just moved!!" Tim left the boat anchored there for the opening day Sunday, and at the end of the day he hoisted Mr. Ed off the boat and onto his car using the Etchells hoist. My sister in law had never had so much fun in her life, nor did she realize that sailors had so much fun. She is a confirmed power boater, and has won the only two races she has ever been in. Quit while you're ahead I told her, it's not always this easy. 🐚

The Lighter Than Air Drifter

In 1982, before the Swiftsure race in Victoria, BC, one of the crew from the boat I was sailing on suggested we find a prank move for the pre race party.

We came up with the idea of the lighter than air drifter, to be paraded through the party with three members of the crew holding it down.

Sounded like it might be funny. At the loft, we made an 18 foot sausage bag out of half ounce nylon, seam taped it together to prevent leaks, and labeled it as a Lighter than air number one, including our sailmakers label, Smokem Sails.

Light leach cord was sewn in three places along the bottom so that we could hold it down. The owner of our boat rented a helium balloon blow up tank, and we waited outside till the party was getting lively, and then blew the bag up. It held air so well the bag almost, but didn't quite, get away from us and float off. So off to the party of 100 people we go, trying to hold this thing down, and walked through to the laughter and delight of the revelers.

Until a sailmaking rival decided to pull out a knife and slice open the sausage bag. Sick Prick. We let go of our handholds and the sucker sailed around the room like the baloon it was, and landed in a heap on the floor.

The crowd booed him. It was not a good business move on his part, and not long after, he closed his doors in Seattle.

I patched the bag up and during the spinnaker run to the finish of the Swiftsure Race, the camera boats came by. The whole crew went below leaving just one crewman on deck lying down on the floor under the wheel, steering. Great shots of no visible people, just a ghost ship sailing along with a sailbag flying from the foredeck. Hit the local sailing rags as an unusual sailing prank.

The lighter than air drifter ended its sailing life as spinnaker repair cloth. 回

Lightning Bugs in Boston

When we were children, my brother and I went to Boston with our folks.

We were new to the other coast and were unfamiliar with lighting bugs. We don't have them here in California, so they captured our attention in the evenings. Behind our grandfathers house was a forest that was a great place to play in the days, and came alive in the night with fireflies.

Ed and I went out one evening with mason jars to capture some of these unusual insects, and got quite a few. We were happy with our catch, and to show our excitement, we brought them inside to show grandpa.

Ed, in a fit of fun, opened the jar and let them out. They were flying around everywhere, and grandpa was pissed. So mad that he ran around the house swatting them with a flyswatter. They died on the wall and glowed for hours.

It looked like a starry night! 回

Molotov Sailors

Years ago, at a major west coast yacht club, a group of the poor boys joined hands and ventured off to the ladies room to "powder their noses".

Several minutes later they reappeared with toilet paper hanging out of their butts, dangling to the floor. The toilet paper was on fire! They danced around, wiggling their tails and when one fire went out, another dancer would help relight it. This went on for several minutes before their respective owners put a stop to it at the risk of being cut off at the bar. Nobody was tossed, but they all had a good laugh before venturing off to the swimming pool for some after hours good times. 🐚

Race You to the Roof!

Big boat series a few years back, shortly after the big Oakland earthquake, "Jeff", one of our crew walked into the bar at Saint Francis YC and found another crewman who was chatting with a tall blond woman.

He walked up to them to say hi, and when she tuned to him she said, "he's telling flat jokes". She wasn't large in that arena, and not too happy about his jokes and said to Jeff "can we get out of here?" Jeff, as she looked like a famous movie star, said but of course!! Off the three of them went walking to Chestnut Street in the marina district for dinner.

Along the way they passed many earthquake damaged buildings, scaffolding set up around them for the rebuilding process. "Jeff" and the blond looked up at one structure when she said "don't you dare me". He looked at her and said "race you to the top"! She took off climbing the scaffolding while he quietly watched. "Jeff" calmly walked over to the construction ladder and was there to give her a hand up at the top.

Dinner at the Chestnut grill was lovely, calm and well served till the flat joke crewman was leaning back and tipped over backwards off his chair.

It got worse from there as dinner digressed, eventually deteriorating into a butter knife fight with the next table full of sailor friends. No one was hurt but the wall took a few hits!

"Jeff" took her home to the room that he shared with the flat joke fellow crewman; who said to them, "do what ever you want, just don't make any noise". They went on to make a bunch of noise and later heard it from the flat joke guy. Who will remain anonymous, as will she.

To protect the guilty. 🐚

Shaken—Not Stirred

Not really a sailing story here, but one of my sailing buds, Bruce, paid a visit to a friend who owned a farm in Queensland, Australia. And on this farm the owner had a bunch of animals, including a pet Kangaroo.

The owner of the farm uttered the famous two words of the American south and said, "Watch this".

He then went to the freezer and pulled out a nearly frozen six pack of Fosters, and placed it in the Kangaroo's pouch. It went about as well as expected. Not well. The Kangaroo freaked out and leapt all over the place, kicking and yowling for a few minutes before finally connecting with Bruce's head. Bruce was stunned to say the least, but vividly remembers the animal leaping all over the farm in distress.

After the Kangaroo had warmed up the beer enough to settle down, the farmer removed the six pack and passed them around to all the laughing bystanders, who opened them up to a spray of well warmed, and shaken, not stirred, beer. 🐚

Slick Goes Astray

A good friend of mine, we'll call him "Mac" to protect the guilty, asked to borrow my J 24 for a collegiate national championship regatta.

My boat was pretty fast and had won the fleet championships several times, and he was kind of begging me to let him use it for the University of Washington team. Sure I said. They were scrambling around for boats for the twenty some schools, and I trusted him. I had sailed with him on his dad's boat when he and his brother were junior sailors.

He and his brother have Olympic medals now

Two days before the racing was to begin, he came by the houseboat to pick up the boat. It was parked on the dock in the back. As he was taking off, I suggested that he take a look at where he was when leaving the narrow channel so he would be able to find his way back to return the boat when the regatta was over. There are hundreds of houseboats in Seattle, and a lot of waterways, so if you don't look, you can miss it.

UW went on to win the regatta. I was happy my boat was a part of the win, as it was a really good J 24. If there is such a thing.

The deal was that all the schools would return the boats to their respective slips, or pull them out at the dry storage for the owners after the racing ended on Monday.

I kind of expected to see the boat back later Sunday evening. It is an hour in from Puget Sound, requiring a trip thru the locks to the fresh water lake. In fact several of the borrowed boats were from the lake. I sort of expected the lake boats to all go through the locks together after the prize letting, and that they mine show up in the early evening.

It was a long wait, and the boat never turned up. I wasn't too worried; he's a good guy and a good sailor so I knew my boat was in good hands. But two days later, Slick still wasn't home.

The next day was thanksgiving; Laurie and I were on our way to a friend's house with our contribution, a big turkey dinner, with dressing, cranberry and all. A typical American T day dinner.

On the way we spotted our J 24 rafted up to a restaurant dock on Lake union.

Shit, I thought, my boats gone AWOL, and with out my permission.

I had Laurie drop me off at the restaurant, and I drove the boat back to its home on our houseboat across the lake.

Three days later, Mac called me up.

Sheepishly, he asked, have you seen your J 24? He apparently had no idea where he had left it and had finally come around to the fact that they had left it at some restaurant somewhere, and didn't remember which one, and needed to come clean.

Probably the result of a big night for the team.

I of course, asked him what was going on, and where the hell is my boat?

I played it up to the max, causing the University of Washington team sailing team captain large amounts of grief and concern. I finally told him where it was after letting him sweat it for a while.

A nice J24 is a valuable boat, even if it is just a J 24. 🐚

The Kiel Canal Funnelator

Sayula II was transiting the Kiel Canal, returning home to Acapulco from Finland after the Whitbread Round the World Race.

Butch had brought his funnelator along for fun.

The Kiel Canal is fairly narrow, so we had a pretty close look at the passing ships. We would sit by the fore hatch, three guys and Vanessa, and wait. A ship would come the other way and Vanessa would pull off her top and shake the girls at the bridge. When the captain came out for a look, Butch and Bobby would stand up, I would lay on the floor of the forepeak and fire off a water balloon. We scored some good hits till the captains started alerting the following ships with warnings. Shortly after, we were getting bags of trash and garbage thrown at us. Seemed a little unfair as we were just using water to give the Euros a bath, and they were using trash cans full of refuse.

At the West end of the Kiel canal, after our funnelator trip, Butch, Bobby, and I were walking along the streets of a small western German town named Brunsbittle, when we spotted a VW Bus with California plates, and a bumpersticker that read "California, land of fruits and nuts". Well, we just had to follow the bus to its end, which turned out to be a brothel. One American and two Brits followed in and found a quite nice gentleman's club; complete with movies and girls who spoke no English, but they were showing off their wares. Drinks were pouring for free as encouragement to partake in the pleasures of the young ladies present.

Movies played on the wall behind the bar, rather graphic movies. At the climax of a movie, our group would burst into wild applause, clapping and cheering loudly.

They were very disappointed in our lack of participation with their trade.

Eventually we found the driver of the bus who was very happy at the time, and he agreed to take us home. He was from Holland, but had been to California and had bought the bus and bumper sticker there.

California, land of fruits and nuts! 🐚

The Night Owls

During the 1985 Big Boat Series, my roommate Bruce, who shall feature often through this book and I returned to our room at the Cow Hollow early. 10:30 PM or so. As we lay in our beds, watching an old cowboy movie, we looked toward each other and said "what the hell are we doing in bed at 10:30 on a Friday night in San Francisco?? Let's go find the crew! So we thought about where they might be, and decided that Henry Africa's would be the most likely watering hole. We got up, put on our worst clothes and went out to hunt them down. Sure enough, there were 6 of the crew there. Hooray! We proceeded to party till closing time, by which time most of our crew had evacuated the place.

Around closing time, the barkeep came up to us and said that one of our crew had left his wallet at the bar, and could we return it to him? Well of course we could. I opened it up to be sure it was one of our guys, and sure enough, it was. He was younger than my roommate and I, but very well to do. Shuffling through his wallet we found stacks of $100.00 dollar bills along with a mass of credit cards. Well, we said, drinks on the house, (there were not too many people there at 1:45 AM.) Spotting the chalkboard behind the bar we saw Stolichnaya Vodka for only $20.00 per bottle! Better yet, below that was Dom Peringon for only $100.00 per bottle! In our cups, we requested one of each. The barkeep looked at me and said," you're not going to do that to your friend, are you? We thought about it for a minute and cancelled the Stoli. But still a round for the crowd.

The next day on the way to the boat, our amigo was trying to find his wallet to pay for his breakfast, but he had to rely on the generosity of his crewmates, of which we were two, for his breakfast. We bought him breakfast with his own money. When we arrived at the boat, I took out his wallet and placed a credit card in each sea boot. One in each pocket of his foulies, one in his crew shirt, and one in the Nav station. All day long on the race course he would put a hand in a pocket and come out with a credit card and say out loud "where the hell was I last night?" Most of the crew were in on it and we all had a good laugh over it on the race course that day. We made him buy us all dinner that night. He is a restaurateur in Los Angeles, and knows all the good places. But the best thing was the Dom. Bruce and I found some femmes on Saturday night that were attracted to the finer things in life, and we were the finer things that night. We all enjoyed the Dom.

Thanks, you know who. 🐚

Movie Star Stockings

My night owl friend, room mate, and fellow sailmaker, was into outrageous behavior. He had a penchant for toe sucking. In unusual locations.

At the 1985 Big Boat Series in San Francisco, we sailed on a new 45 foot Frers boat with a well known TV star and her husband. Once again, no names here.

At a very nice Italian restaurant, during our crew dinner, I heard a yelp from her, and a "what is that?" Apparently my roommate had gone under the dinner table and was going after a little toe sucking. But there was a small problem. She was wearing panty hose.

Here he is, on the floor under the table, chewing through the toes of her stockings. He then went on to suck on her toes with the crew watching for her reaction. She handled it quite well, and as she is more of a comedian than most, and laughed it off.

With a blush.

He went on to perform in many restaurants around the country, and world. 🔯

The Running of the Cougars

Ah, the running of the Cougars... A fine tradition!!

Each year, the night before the Ensenada race from Newport Beach, Ca, Bahia Corinthian YC has a pre race party that can't be missed. Sailors from all over come down a day early just to attend this once a year fiesta/send off. Even if they're not sailing.

They come from far and near to rub shoulders with their sailing buddies and swap new stories, as well as rehash old ones. Meet any new crew members on their boat, and generally get prepared for the grueling, long spinnaker run to the cozy little town of Ensenada. A short 120 miles away.

And to get drunk as skunks. Sleeping on the boat is the best option, as it's a mere 3 minute stagger down the dock-unless you need to stop for a chunder.

The highlight of this event is not the sailing but the running of the Cougars.

Apparently the desperate housewives of Orange County have discovered this event, as they too come from far and wide to see what kind of fun they can find and see if they can get lucky. They come early as they have learned what sailors do at these things, and how bad it can get. They stand together in small groups and select their prey. Then they move in for the kill. Many a sailor has been late for dock out, with only a small hangover compared to the ones not chosen that stayed late.

The Chicago Mac race has a similar pre race ritual party with a different twist. Each crewperson is given a wrist band that admits them to the pre race party at the Chicago Yacht Club.

An hour before the party, the line up of non wristband holders forms and stretches out to the street and beyond. All the cute little Chicago debutants looking for fun with visiting sailors are there, to get the sailors to buy them drinks, and take it from there. The sailors are all too willing to do this, but the girls have to get in first.

Jesus god, most of the Chicago Debs are almost as good looking as the Georgia peaches down Atlanta way, but with just a little less sun.

Enter a good owner. A good owner is one who buys two wrist bands for each of his crew so they can walk the line and choose which deb they want to spend the evening with. He can give her the band and she's in and he's a hero.

Take it from there.

Care to see my yacht honey?

Another fun part of the Mac is the Pink Pony Bar on Mackinaw Island. The Deb's come up there from Chicago to party with the first to finish crew, all night.

Nice to be on a ninety footer for this race. 🐚

Bloody Eye

One year on the 135 mile Swiftsure race, run out of Victoria, BC. Canada, we were sailing on a Swan 441. Half the crew was from Seattle with the other half from Southern California.

Obvious how the watches would sort out.

We had a great beat out to the lightship, and were doing quite well. On the way out, Cecil, who was a stunt double in Hollywood at the time, showed me a bottle of fake blood. Very realistic stuff. He said he was going to RF the owner at some point in the race, with a chuckle.

Two thirds through the race while we were spinnakering back to Victoria in the afternoon, Cecil came lurching out of the hatch with a knife in his hand, and the fake blood dripping from his eye. He shouted "my eye-my eye" The So Cal boys knew Cecil, and were in on it, but the owner and the Seattle watch almost had heart attacks. The owner fainted. We all had a great laugh, and after reviving the owner we cleaned up the "blood". 🐚

Cold Sea Boots

During the Whitney Series on *Robon*, a C&C 61, we had some-one on the boat that was really not a favorite. He was from the east coast, and just didn't fit in with the Santa Monica poor-boys. Constantly pissing the crew off with tales of his exaggerated adventures that we doubted. The Santa Monica poorboys decided something needed to be done. We thought about it for a while and came up with ideas.

During a race around an island off Los Angeles, we rinsed the inside of his boots with a little water, and put them into the freezer while he was off watch. We then put them back before waking him up. He spent 20 minutes trying to figure out what was up with his boots while we chastised him about getting up on deck on time to help jibe the starcut. Is this how you sail on that other coast we asked? He was not too pleased with us left coasters to say the least. He got a little mouthy about it at first, as his boots were frozen, and second, "jibe a starcut?"

He gave us a ration of grief, but the poorboys didn't take grief well. It was apparent that we had to carry it further.

We put a few cups of powdered sugar into his sleeping bag. When the bag warms up with body heat, it results in white sticky goo. Got him good and he never gave us any shit again.

Nobody used his sleeping bag either. 🐚

The Florida Bratwurst Prank

At one very raucous pre race party in Fort Lauderdale, "Jeff" had a few drinks and came up with a fun idea.

He snatched a Bratwurst from the buffet table, went into the bathroom, and then came running out screaming oh my god, oh my god it hurts!

He had stuck the Bratwurst out of his fly and zipped it up with the thing sticking out. Children ran, women fainted, and the men just laughed. He was one of the consummate prank-

sters of the time, and features often in this little book. Anony-
mously of course! 🐚

Toilet Seats

Twas night before Transpac a few years back, try 1977, when
Timmy and Bobby snuck aboard Hawkeye. Hawkeye is a
Bruce King bilge boarder that was really hot in its day along
with its little sister, Terrorist.

These two pirates stole Hawkeyes toilet seat on the eve of
the 2225 mile race, and laughed all the way to Hawaii. The
Hawk crowd had their own little private Idaho. Most of the
guys weren't shy about going off the transom, but the older
owner had more than a few delicate moments perched on the
stern pulpit.

Everyone got a good laugh over that one, till Hawaii, where
the Hawk crew retaliated by removing Timmy and Bobbie's
steering wheel the night before they were to leave on their de-
livery back to California. 🐚

Wired Propeller

Then there was the Big Boat Series where the Hawk crew
wired the Martec prop on Swiftsure closed. Swiftsure couldn't
figure out what was going on, as the boat wouldn't go, and
they missed the start. 🐚

Greg'sBlanket

We were flying across the sea of Cortez on an eighty foot M
boat named Sirius II, doing about 14 knots. Flying? One of
the crew, Greg Palmer was asleep in the aft cabin. It was late
afternoon and Jeff was off watch bored, and looking for something to do. He found a bucket and a 30 foot length of line,
and tied one end to a corner of Greg's blanket. He then ran the
other end of the line out the hatch to a bucket and tossed the
bucket over the side.

Wow! That blanket came up and out so fast poor Greg never knew what hit him. Few were in on it, but watching that purple blanket fly out of the hatch was a thing to behold! It had everyone in tears laughing. Jeff had to buy the owner a replacement blanket and bucket; it was worth every penny to see Greg's face and surprise! The crew chipped in on the replacement blanket!

A bit later that same day, Jeff was asleep in the folded up jib on the foredeck when a flying fish landed on him. It seemed like an opportunity. He tied some light line to the tail, and dangled it down the center hatch right over the sleeping Abo's nose. He would touch it to his nose and then pull it away as he swatted at it. The whole watch was ringed around the hatch laughing. It was a stinky fish too. After about ten minutes of this, Abo caught on and waited for the drop, grabbed the line and was almost able to pull him down the hatch! 🐚

The Drink Tickets

The son of P.I.T.C.H regatta is held in Everett, Washington over the three day Labor Day weekend. We were sailing the first J 35 on the west coast, and doing quite well. New boat, new sails, racing against older I.O.R boats, and having our way with the competition.

Parties every night needed drink tickets, for some fee of course. One of our crew waited till the ticket seller left for a bathroom break and snagged a roll of said tickets, and began passing them out to his friends in the bar. Lots of them. After 30 minutes of this, the Yacht club began to catch on. So the crewman handed the tickets to the owner of the boat to pass on to his friends, customers, and other crews. His friends were very grateful, thinking it was a business expense and enjoyed many "free" drinks on the owner. Till the Yacht Club manager came up to him, took the tickets and tossed him out.

Poor guy never knew how this happened. 🐚

Paquita's Knitting

Ramon Carlin's wife Paquita came along with us on *Sayula II* for the first leg of the Whitbread Round the World race from Portsmouth England to Capetown. It was a slow one and she was very bored, as were we all. She had brought along her knitting gear, and spent most every day below knitting. She had a plan. For me.

Paquita spent weeks knitting a little pillow, about six inches square. One day just before the finish in Cape Town, she called me down below. I didn't know what to expect, but she had a pair of scissors and I was running scared. She cornered me anyway, sat me down and lopped off half of my very long hair and stuffed her little pillow with it. It was a nice pillow, with a Mexican pattern on it. Everyone was laughing at my expense as my neck and head got sunburned!

She mailed her little pillow to my mother in California from Cape Town, who was pleased that someone finally got me to cut my hair! 🐚

Pywacket and the Coasties

Greg Hedrick was delivering Roy Disney's Santa Cruz 70 *Pywacket* home from Honolulu after Transpac.

Motoring through the Pacific high, a coast guard cutter appeared from nowhere and stopped them. The coasties launched one of their chase boats and proceeded over for an impromptu inspection.

When they arrived in their Aluminum boat, Greg took one look at it and said no way were they getting anywhere close to his perfect boat. He had seen the Midwest coasties in action before. They went away and returned with a rubber boat and were allowed to board, guns drawn.

Do you know whose boat this is Greg asked? They shrugged and asked to see enough life jackets for the crew, which were produced. Now, Greg, the *Pywacket* captain, is quite a large guy with a great sense of humor, but when the coasties asked him which one of the life jackets fit him, that was enough. He snapped. He told them to get off his boat. He then asked if the head coastie had any children or grandchildren. Why yes he did. Greg then said "well don't ever think about taking them to Disneyland! 🐚

A Ghost Story

When I was a child my father would take us to Catalina Island. Santa Catalina is a 20 mile long 5 mile wide island, 18 miles off the coast of Los Angeles. Our family would go over for weekends all summer long.

My dad loved sailing and instilled sailing in the two of us kids. (My mother hated it). My dad was also a member of the MIT sailing club in 1939.

He would come home from work on Friday nights during the summer, pack us up and we would race down to the boat. My dad, mother, my 7 years older brother and I would then sail the 18 miles to the island. On an eighteen foot hard chine plywood boat!! I was quite small, so I didn't take up much space and played on the floor with a percolator coffee pot. In the morning we kids would wake up on a mooring at the Isthmus on the island, my dad sleeping after having sailed all night to get us there. We would hang out on the mooring for the weekend then sail back home to L.A. on Sunday.

I have many fond memories of our time on the island. My brother would chum for local island fish and shoot them with his bow and arrow. He was pretty good at it too. We would walk the rocks during minus tides and pick off Abalones which dad would clean, pound, and fry up. He also had a pancake flag that went up every Sunday morning. Fellow club members would come by for my dad's famous pancakes, and we had company for hours. He would make them a special drink. The Phillips screwdriver.

Made with the traditional Vodka, he used Tang, powdered Orange juice.

A perfect Phillips screwdriver!

When I was a bit older, 8 or so, we got a much bigger boat. A 28 footer! It was a seabird yawl, and we would repeat the

93

process all summer long. Sail over; pick up a mooring then sail home on Sunday.

As I got older I was allowed to sleep ashore with my yacht club friends. During the night, we might be attacked by wild boars raiding the trash cans for food, or the occasional Buffalo cruising through the camp. We cowered in our sleeping bags all night long, terrified.

My dad also had a 45 caliber army pistol. He brought it out one day and showed me how to shoot it. I aimed at the cliffs and let her rip.

Sucker knocked my 8 year old ass over the side! He had a string tied to the gun so I couldn't lose it. I'm guessing you can't get away with that these days!

Once every summer dad would sail home with another family and leave my brother and me on our boat for two or three weeks with our mother. Another family stayed on their boat as well, and their dad did the same sail home to return later with my dad. We kids had the run of this part of the island for two or three weeks. The two dads would then come back to join us and we would all sail back home on our respective boats. Sometimes all the kids on the same boat for fun. After this 28 footer, we had a series of larger boats and spent a ton of time on Catalina Island.

Many years later I sailed on a very long ocean race. A very long ocean race. Upon my return to Los Angeles, I was offered a position in Seattle, which I accepted, and moved up north to start a new sail loft and a new life.

In 1995 during the construction of my new boat, my father was diagnosed with cancer. Terminal cancer. It was really hard, and he eventually died.

He was cremated per his wishes. He had been living in Brookings, Oregon, and his wife wanted to dump his ashes off his boat into the sea he loved so much, again per his wishes, but she didn't want to wait for my brother and me to get there. I think she was eager to fulfill his wishes. She and I agreed to coincide our services at ten AM on a Sunday morning. I launched my Olson 30 in Seattle, and with a bottle of Champagne and a dozen roses, motored out into Puget Sound.

At precisely 9:45, a seabird yawl motored out of the breakwater. They hoisted sails and began sailing along on starboard tack. Right across my bow. I was drifting, just sitting on the bow of the Olson 30 with the engine off. At exactly ten o'clock, they crossed my bow. The helmsman, steering exactly the way my dad did, leaned over and waved to me, hello or good by. I'm not sure. At ten AM. I tossed the roses at him. I will forever think that he was saying good-bye.

He was a good dad and gave us a good growing up in sailing. 🕸

Zaca, a Seabird yawl

Herman in his pool boat

Change for a Nickel Anyone?

A good friend, Dan, was a yacht broker in Seattle and bought a lot of sails from Sails by Watts. He was a very staunch supporter of my fledgling little company, and I owe him a note of gratitude for our success in Seattle.

He is a bit of an odd duck though.

He recruited me to provide sails for, and sail the very first C&C 33 in Seattle. It was his company owned boat, and he named it *Shiva*, which I'm thinking is a Hindu goddess. A few months later, another one of his customers bought a new C&C 33 and went with a different brand of sails.

No biggie, this happens. So when the rival sailmaker came up from Los Angeles to sail against us, Dan couldn't resist a wager. The other boat was named *Burgundy*. So the bet was on. If they won, a bottle of Burgundy for them, and if we won, a bottle of "Shiva's Regal" for us.

We had a great crew party with the "Shiva's Regal"!

Our next project was a C&C 1/2 tonner Dan named *Island* after the country he's from, Iceland.

I couldn't sail a major regatta on the boat with him due to a previous commitment to another boat, so I had my sailmaker brother come up to Seattle to sail with Dan on *Island*. About an hour before we were supposed to leave the dock, my brother Ed strolls up to me and asks, "what's up with Dan?" How was I to know? Why do you ask? Ed said that Dan was asking everyone on his boat, the next boat, and any boats nearby for change for a nickel. Ed thought this was just a little odd, and did I have any suggestions? No, just play along was all I could come up with.

And keep both feet on the floor.

Did I say that Dan was an odd duck?

It was a two day regatta and Dan had found his pennies. On the way out to the start of the first race, Dan was throwing his "I Ching" pennies around the cockpit, much to the disbelief and dismay of my very conservative brother and the rest of the crew, whom I had supplied for the most part.

"What have I gotten myself into here?" Ed thought to himself.

My brother is pretty darned conservative, just not on the race course. But they did go on to win their class in the regatta, just as the I Ching had predicted!

Island was a relatively unfinished boat with a large unpainted aft bulkhead, just forward of the rudder post. Dan was a mite frugal. We, Ted Allison and I, while delivering the boat to the San Juan Islands decided that the wall was a potential unpainted Andy Warhol canvas, so we went on to add a little bit of art each day. Lipstick kisses from the ladies, smudges of this and that, duct tape, grease, fingerprints, bits of colored spinnaker repair tape, smudges of blood and whatever else struck our fancy. Art deco. Turned out to be more like a Picasso. We even taped some of our winch handles to the wall so that the crew had go look for them later for the mid-summers regatta in Canada.

While delivering the boat home to Seattle after racing for a week in the cold white North, Ted rigged up the spin sheets to the tiller so that he and his wife Carolyn could steer from the foredeck, get naked, and do their thing. Double handed.

It was a spinnaker run down Puget Sound to Seattle, and they were getting busy on the bow. The breeze came up, but they were distracted. The boat rolled down on a puff, and they were almost cast out through the lifelines into Puget Sound! All naked, and all.

Dan's next boat was an Express 27, designed by Carl Schumacher. I'm not even sure it had a name. We just called it *Picasso* and did our interior painting thing. In 1983 we did the short course Swiftsure with the first Mylar spinnaker in the northwest. Now there was another good idea. Mylar spinnakers. Not!

We managed to make it around the weather mark in good shape for a little light weight boat in 25 knots of wind, and were anticipating the 30 mile fast spinnaker run back to Victoria. But in the afternoon a fog bank came up behind us, and Dan, as the navigator, was asked to get bearings on the prominent points of interest and plot them. We were on port jibe heading for Canada when the fog enveloped us. It was blowing 20 k, and we couldn't see 3 boat lengths ahead of us. We knew we were getting on towards the Canadian shore, so we kept a good eye out for bounce back waves from the six foot swell. Little did we know that the ebb tide had pushed us to the North, or left, closer to the shoreline than expected.

The first inkling of trouble was the noticeable lack of bounce back waves.

We kept a sharp eye out for the shore to appear from the fog to our left, when to our dismay and surprise, there were trees to the right of us! We had sailed into a cove on Vancouver Island. Quickly, we jumped to get the spinnaker down, only to have one of the crew let the main halyard go instead.

Bummer, as we were approaching a lee shore, in a cove. Needless to say, we got the plastic fantastic down and the main back up in time to avoid the worst case scenario. We went offshore for ten minutes before gathering our courage enough to reset the spinnaker. The rest of the leg was jibe offshore for ten, and back in for ten till we could see shore. It was really foggy and dark, and we were sort of lost. But seeing the shore pop out at us every twenty minuets was comforting. Nearing race rocks, the turn for the finish, we spotted the lights of Victoria. What we didn't know was that we were seeing the lights over a low spot of land just short of Race Passage. We jibed in till someone noticed the depth shoaling up! Oops, a quick jibe out in eight feet of water, and a quick check of the chart set us right. Damn, another cove for us to sail into. We did get through the passage in time, and were headed for the finish some eight miles off at a good clip when we heard a loud bang and the boat stopped. A log? A flashlight showed that we had indeed hit a six inch diameter log which was folded and pinned on the front of the keel. No amount of backing down would dislodge it. After much discussion, we pushed the thing off with the spinnaker pole, and off we went. All in all, a busy, interesting race. And we did well too! 🐚

Cold Hands

In 1974, a few of us were living on *Sayula II* in Lymington, England.

Somehow we got invited to sail in Scotland on a brand new Ron Holland one tonner back when they were 36 footers. Sounded like spontaneous fun to us 23 year olds.

Butch, Bobby and I drove up from Lymington to Glasgow, with a stop at a lovely town called Clovelli, which is perched on a hillside West of Bristol. You have to walk down a long stairway to town, and for groceries, there was a tram.

We were on our way to Glasgow to help launch, rig the boat, and deliver it down the river to Greenock, and to sail Clyde race week.

The owner, Bill McKai, built the boat in Glasgow quite quickly in something less than high tech stuff. Phil Holland was there to oversee it all and take care of the boat. Phil... Nice job Phil...

The firth of Clyde is a narrow channel, or loch, and the wind blows down it from Ireland. This happened to be a particularly windy year. Races in the 30's every day. Bill could have done a bit better job of building it, as it leaked. A lot. But it was fast. We did Clyde race week and had a glorious time as well as doing pretty well.

We must have been OK, as Bill asked us to sail the one ton worlds in Torquey with him. Cool. So we stayed in the UK a few extra months to do it.

After Scotland, driving back to Lymington, we celebrated at many pubs along the way, finding some nice extracurricular activities as well.

The worlds rolled around, and having a Scottish owner, we three had to stay on the boat—to our horror. The sailing was great, but in the end we wound up just at the one third point of the fleet. So what, we were there, and not in Finland with the rest of the *Sayula* group.

Each night after sailing, we and lots of other racers would walk to the disco, a few blocks from the marina, and do what you do at discos. Every night Phil would fall asleep on a couch. Perhaps pass out might be more accurate. The bouncers would try to toss him, but we calmed them down and said he was just tired from a long day of sailing, and just needed a little nap. We would take care of him. Seemed to work as they left him alone after.

The problem was that the boat leaked so much from the beating it had taken in Scotland that in the morning it would have a fair amount of water, and it would take us half an hour to bail it out. We thought that if it continued in this way, with the windy sailing we were having, we might all have to swim out of the boat one night. So we lit upon a plan. Each night we would take turns lashing a hand to the floorboards so that when the water got up to his elbow the lucky sleeper would wake up. Worked like a charm as the water there is very cold, but even then, every night there was bailing going on.

I'm thinking the boat was used for firewood after.
Unless it was too wet. 🪢

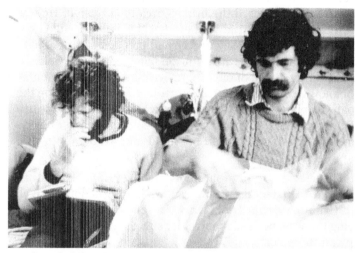

Butch and Phil Holland on Billycan.

Firecrackers at Night

Transpac 1973 was a windy year. We, the Santa Monica mafia, AKA the poor boys, sailed it on a C&C 61 named *Robon* out of Newport Beach.

There were many in our crew who have gone on to be very high echelon sailors in their classes, and some who flamed out. I don't know which category I fit into, but some of the names you will still see in sailing magazines and articles.

Transpac was windy enough to require twice-daily trips up the rig to check the wire halyards and the masthead blocks. On the second day out we were reaching along with our starcut (remember them) when Mike went forward to check on things at the end of the pole. While he was on the bow, the afterguy shackle parted and the pole smashed onto his face crushing his lips and damaging his teeth. We quickly pulled him aft and laid him down to recoup. Blood was everywhere. Those same poorboys decided that sewing his lip up was the right thing to do and that fell upon me as the resident sail maker. We filled him with Scotch (to numb the pain) and filled ourselves for courage. I brought out the sail repair kit complete with waxed twine, and then dosed the broken area to cleanse it. He was pretty apprehensive and wild eyed at this point. I pulled out a rusty curved sailmaking needle and prepped him up. Blood was everywhere still, when out the hatch comes the voice of reason in the name of one George Griffith. Many of you may not know George, but he was our resident curmudgeon on the boat. George was instrumental in the design of the Lapworth 36, and the Cal 40. Many of the concepts and ideas for these landmark boats came from his mind and were input to Bill Lapworth.

He took one look at what we were going to do to poor Mike, and said, "Hold on there children, what are you doing?" Well Mr. Griffith, we're just going to sew up old Mikey here. George, being the seasoned sailor and elder statesman he was, stepped up and stopped us.

He then proceeded to put on a butterfly bandage, and taped him up. The owner of *Robon's* son applied copious quantities of vitiman E oil for the rest of the trip, and by the time we finished the Transpac, you could barely see any sign of damage.

One of our crew, in a fit of mischievousness, tossed a lit package of firecrackers into the crew cockpit at 2:00 am. These suckers went off for 3 minutes and scared the bandage right off of Mikey's lip and the bejesus out of the trimmers. Imagine being on deck half asleep at 2 AM and a package of firecrackers blowing up at your feet!

The whole pit crew came down to beat the shit out of us, but as we were grinders too, it became a bit of a Hawaiian standoff. It was filmed, but I have no idea where it might be these days.

Mike grew a moustache to cover the tiny scar. 🐚

Insight Stories

Once upon a time in Florida, a group of us from California sailed a Nelson/Marek 36 called *Insight*. It was a crappy, uncomfortable little boat for offshore sailing. It was fast though, and we sailed it fairly well. Well enough to come second in the S.O.R.C. Morgan yachts built it in record time.

Too fast.

When we arrived in Clearwater from California, the owner, Ben, took us home to his house to relax and clean up. He then brought us into a guest bedroom to introduce us to the 6 foot 6 inch 280 pound paid hand. He was flopped on the bed with the flu, and Ben said, "Look at him, he's like a beached whale!" He is well known in southern California, so no names here.

We kind of got the boat ready. On the way out to the start of the first race, the Boca Raton 100 miler, we were bolting on pad eyes on the port side for the jib top leads, as well as the other needed deck parts. The boat was just a bit late to say the least.

It was a very early carbon boat, and the factory didn't have the expertise to build this type of boat. They made some mistakes along the way. One of which was not isolating the carbon from the stainless steel stanchions and bolts. Norman found this out the hard way when he went to pee off the transom and accidently dribbled on the stern pulpit and got the shock no man wants. He has only one son to this day. But we all have a vivid memory in our minds as we remember the scream!

The second long distance race, the Saint Pete/Ft Lauderdale race, goes out around Key West, into the Gulf Stream, and then North to Fort Lauderdale. My watch was off sleeping at 6 AM, when we awoke with a start. It was blowing 30 knots, we were bouncing around, and something smelled really bad. Really bad. Turns out our experienced paid hand had gone up to abuse the head in a legendary way. He blew up the holding tank bladder.

Apparently the Cubans who built the boat were too lazy to climb down the ladder to use the shop facilities, and just used the boat head. We awoke to turds floating in the bilge, as there were no floorboards.

The stench of two months of Cubans was overbearing. Grabbing our jackets, we ran. Out to the weather rail where the on watch said "you're not due for two hours". I said "I'm out here because there's something really ugly going on down there. Just take a look". It was awful.

I looked over at Norman and said, "Breakfast?" and offered to go down and get Frosted Flakes, milk, bowls and spoons. Enough for all.

There were only 6 of us crew total. The owner told his paid hand, in no uncertain terms, that if he wasn't smart enough to turn the head handle to overboard, then he had to clean it up. So it really meant only four of us on the rail for breakfast.

I spent two minutes hyperventilating, put my hand under my eyes so as not to see the floor, and ran below to return with Frosted Flakes and bowls. When I made it back outside, I proceeded to puke off the transom, then went over and sat up on the rail to recover next to Norman, having accomplished half my goal, as well as making room for more food. Norman says, "No problem my nose doesn't work anymore anyway." and he went for the rest of the kit. He blanched when he came out, but he brought the rest of the stuff. So here we are four hardy hands sitting up on the weather rail in 30 knots of wind, a number 4 Genoa and double reefed main pounding up the Gulf Stream. Laughing at our hand and eating cereal, which is being blown off of our spoons into the next person aft's bowl. Just then, out through the fore hatch comes this large bladder being tossed over the side. To be followed shortly by the rest of what ever was left in the head. The bladder caught on the lifelines and hung there like a dead seal for the two minutes it took our rep to finish puking and disengage it.

Our IBNA rep spent two hours cleaning up the mess in between bouts of throwing up in the cockpit, and not getting his Frosted Flakes.

We won our class in this race despite the antics of our IBNA rep.

He spent two days cleaning the inside in Fort Lauderdale.
🐚

Roo and the Fish

The last day of the 1998 Mexorc in Puerto Vallarta, we were motoring out to the start on *Zephryus*, an RP 77.

One of the crew spotted a struggling Porpoise who was trapped in a net, and quite probably dying. Seeing this, Roo our Kiwi IBNA. rep, grabbed a large knife and put it in his teeth like the pirate of Bandaras Bay. He jumped into the water and swam over to the fish. Trying to cut the net away, the fish wouldn't hold still long enough for him to get it done. Enter one of our Mexican kids, Odean, who jumped into the water and swam over to Roo.

Odean started stroking the head and snout, speaking to the suffering fish gently in Spanish. The fish eventually calmed down long enough for Roo to cut the net away. When Roo was finished, the Porpoise swam away returning to its family and brought the whole crowd back a few minutes later. They swam a few laps around the boat jumping and having fun as Porpoise do, and took off while we motored away to the starting area.

Smart fish they are.

We won our first race of the series that day, Karma, perhaps.

Returning to the marina later that day, the pod reappeared for some more laps, jumps, and lots of squealing. We all felt pretty good about what Roo did.

It even made a major sailing magazine! 🐚

The IBNA. "In Us They Trust"

In the early seventies and into the eighties, a group of radicals formed a labor union made up of sailors who took care of their owner's boats. Probably started by Barry Constant and Greg Tuxworth. They used the initials IBNA. You will have to read between the lines for what it really means. Their logo was a crossed mop and winch handle with the words "In us they trust" beneath. There were shirts made and distributed to only the IBNA group. They agreed to share these rare shirts with select friends and crew. You would find these guys at the SORC. Cowes week, Admirals cup, and as far south as Southern Cross cup in Sydney. Basically, every major regatta where racers congregated. More so to this day.

These are the guys who prepped and put the boats together before big races. They took them apart and cleaned them up after racing, and then prepared the boats for shipping home.

They glued them back together after collisions, hosed them out after racing when the paid crew went off to the bar not thinking about the worker bees that made their next day possible. After, they put the boat back together; they took the sails to the loft, replaced halyards, and rebuilt winches, made sure the bottom cleaner was scheduled for the AM. They just worked on and on. They are the true heroes, and there are just as many today who work just as hard and do the same dirty jobs behind the scenes.

The IBNA, in us they trust! 🔄

The Surfboard

During the Clipper Cup in Hawaii in 1982, they still used the old offshore championship format. Two buoy races followed by a medium distance race, another buoy race, and then a long distance race, which in Hawaii means the round the state race. It's pretty grueling sailing as it's usually windy in Hawaii, but at least it is warm and sticky down below.

We were sailing *Tomahawk*, a red Holland 40 owned by John Arens.

Before the start of the round the state race, it was pissing down rain from a nearby hurricane. The crews were hunkered down under the Hawaii YC balcony getting their clothes wet and dreading going out into the downpour. Eventually we had to wave our families good by and get on with it. It wasn't too long after the start that the rain stopped and it became fun again. Half of our crew was from Seattle, WA and didn't mind the rain as much as the Southern California guys who had perhaps never been sailing in the rain.

The start takes you out around Diamond Head, and around Oahu to port, Kauai to port then on to Niihau, to port. Then on to the big island, Hawaii, for a windy thrash up the volcanic coast before finally easing off with spinnakers up towards Molokai, and on to the finish in Honolulu.

In the early morning hours, in lee of Niihau, we were beating into 8 knots of wind on port tack chasing the Nelson Marek 41 *Brook Anne*. I happened to be driving and looking to weather for puffs when one of our crew spotted a surfboard floating a few hundred yards to weather. Ready-about time. We went the hundred yards then tacked again to pick it up. It was a nice little short board (if you like short boards) and in good shape by a well known local shaper. It was taken aboard and put down below in the bow near the head. When the owner, John, got up and went forward to use the head he saw the board and read Doug Weber, the boat captain, the riot act. We could hear him saying, "Doug, I told you to take everything off this boat but you brought a surfboard?" The board had a leash on it and someone from my watch told John that we had to cut off a severed ankle!

John went below for a while after that.

The good news is that the tack towards the beach got us past *Brook Anne*! ✇

What Shall We Do with the Drunken Sailor?

Whidbey Island race week in Oak Harbor, WA is a fun regatta. It's well known in the Pacific North West as "adult summer camp". Adults get to be kids again, party like animals all night long, throw up late at night, and go sailing the next day only to start the fun all over again the next evening.

And go head first bowling too.

One of my crew we'll call "Jim" (name changed to protect the guilty here) was staying at another one of my crew's house on the island. Seems that they had a horrific party when they got home one night. Rum bottles everywhere, and plenty of drunks unable to drive home. Because of all the people, or perhaps because he was drunk, "Jim" couldn't find a bed or a place to sleep. He wound up sleeping in a wheelbarrow that he somehow managed to get into the house.

The next morning we left the dock early enough for a couple of practice tacks, as we all do. "Jim" was the Genoa trimmer on my Olson 30. After the first tack "Jim" said "excuse me" and politely and quietly leaned over the side and tossed up whatever was left in his stomach. The home owner had his own issues as well, but was older and better able to hold his liquor. Probably should have tossed his cookies as well because he was right up next to useless all day long. We did somehow manage to work through our deficiencies and pull out a win. In fact, despite our crew's partying tactics, we were boat of the week, winning every race, a Chelsea clock and GPS to boot.

"Jim" also crewed for us at the J24 nationals in San Francisco in 1983.

Unfortunately for us, the evening before the practice day was his 21st birthday. As a birthday present, the whole crew bought him 21 shots of tequila at the Saint Francis YC bar. You can probably see this one coming.

We later drug him down to my J24 and tossed him into the forepeak with a bottle of water. He neither knew nor cared. The next day was a practice day and we drug him out of the bow for breakfast, thinking pancakes might help, but at least he didn't puke on my cushions in the night. We let him sleep it off in the YC lounge till it was time to leave the dock. "Jim" went right back to his Gopher hole in the bow and slept while we were tuning with another boat. On the approach to the weather mark, we had to roust him out for the set. He was our bow guy after all, and he had to do his thing up there in frontierland. Afterwards he went back to sleep on the floor. We woke him up for sets, jibes and takedowns which he managed despite his huge hangover. 🕸

THE END

Lightning Source UK Ltd.
Milton Keynes UK
UKOW06f1053210515

252013UK00012B/271/P